# PRAISE FOR

MW01063088

*"Dive into this gift of a book and you too can discover pearls of wisdom and buried treasure in the ocean of your soul. Tonia's wisdom sings from the pages with a mermaid's tale that simply delights the senses. I love it!"*

~Ali Day, creator of www.wiseowloracle.com

*"Tonia has done it again! In her book Mermaids: An Empath and Introvert's Guide to Riding the Waves of Life, she dives deeper, sharing messages and ideas that soothe our souls. I love a "How To". In an information heavy world, it's only half the picture. Both a practical, hands-on book and a creative, imaginative metaphysical read. Simply beautiful! Dive in and fall deeply in love with the world of Mermaids."*

~Damien Munro, Heal Your Life® Teacher Trainer for Australia & New Zealand, www.damienmunro.com

*"A superb storyteller, Tonia beautifully awakens an inner desire to dive fully into our own lives. A gentle and quirky book with an essential message that you will refer back to for years."*

~Patricia J. Crane, Ph.D., Author of *Ordering from the Cosmic Kitchen: The Essential Guide to Powerful, Nourishing Affirmations* and Master Trainer, Heal Your Life® programs
www.drpatriciacrane.com

"*Mermaids: An Empath and Introvert's Guide to Riding the Waves of Life* shares the importance of valuing the energy of yin and yang in us all. When we are in balance within ourselves and with our world around us we feel more connected and optimistic about life. This book offers incredible strategies and tools to support the transformation of our body, mind and spirit."

~Sneha Shah and Shashank Gupta, Founder Directors of Isra Centre for Training and Development, www.isra.co.in

"*Igniting and accepting the energy of the divine feminine is both empowering to ourselves and to those we love most in our world. In her book, Mermaids: An Empath and Introvert's Guide to Riding the Waves of Life, Tonia beautifully shares a message relevant to us all. A delightfully intoxicating book that keeps you humming long after you have finished reading.*"

~Sunny Dawn Johnston; Spiritual teacher, Psychic medium and Author of *Invoking the Archangels* and *The Love Never Ends,* www.sunnydawnjohnston.com

"*In Mermaids: An Empath and Introvert's Guide to Riding the Waves of Life,* we dive deep with author, Tonia Browne, as she takes us on a journey into the depths of our soul, awakening the mermaid spirit in all of us! Packed with tools and resources to help navigate the yin and yang within us, this book is a one-of-a-kind treasure."

~Shanda Trofe, Founder of Spiritual Writers Network and Transcendent Publishing, Bestselling Author of *Authorpreneur,* www.shandatrofe.com

# Mermaids

## An Empath And Introvert's Guide to Riding The Waves of Life

## TONIA BROWNE

MERMAIDS

An Empath and Introvert's Guide to Riding the Waves of Life

By Tonia Browne

Copyright © 2019. Tonia Browne. All rights reserved. No part of this publication may be reproduced, distributed, or transmitted in any form or by any means, including photocopying, recording, or other electronic or mechanical methods, without the prior written permission of the publisher, except in the case of brief quotations embodied in critical reviews and certain other noncommercial uses permitted by copyright law.

Transcendent Publishing
PO Box 66202
St. Pete Beach, FL 33736
www.TranscendentPublishing.com

Transcendent
Publishing

ISBN-13: 978-0-9600501-6-1

Front cover: Artist Marco Busoni www.marcobusoni.net

Photographer of Author: Jase White

This book comes from my imagination, life experiences and information I have gained through my work and research. I hope that it encourages you to dive deep into your own life so that you can experience it with more ease and joy. This is not a replacement for medical advice, therapy or other professional services. While I offer suggestions, the decision to take them is at your discretion. Do they feel right and appropriate for you and your situation? If you are unsure, consult a medical, health or other competent professional before adopting the suggestions in this book. There are many professionals offering life-jackets to keep us afloat in times of need.

*Dedicated to the yin and yang of life*

*and*

*everything in between.*

# CONTENTS

# THE SONG

So gently she sang,

warning of the perils of what was to come and of the beauty
that can be.

They didn't listen,

they were only captivated by her beauty,

the outward shine of her glorious heart,

dazzled by her allure and mistaking her wisdom for wiles.

They did not heed her words but came closer,

unchanged by the gifts she offered,

unaltered by the chance of change,

continuing as before with the desire to take

and to claim her as their own.

But she was more powerful and would not be tamed.

And now,

the mermaids come together and sing again.

This time they cannot fail

to give the gifts they want to share.

They sprinkle their sparkle on the human form

engaging an audience ready to shine,

mesmerising and stirring a memory in each high priestess,

reminding a new generation of who they really are

and of their power to transform

our age.

**Tonia Browne**

# Message From The Author

*"The cure for anything is salt water ..."*

*— Isak Dinesen*

## Dear You,

After writing *Spiritual Seas: Diving into Life*, where I share twelve strategies to ride the waves of life with more joy and ease, I found myself called once again to the turquoise seas. This came as no surprise, as the water has much to teach us about life on this earthly plane, and clearly it had more to offer me as well. It was in these waters that I became aware of the murmur of the mermaids.

Mermaids have been around for eons, imparting their wisdom in the hope that we will act on it for the highest good of all. Never has humanity needed these mystical beings more; indeed, they are the keepers of the sagacity needed to transform our age.

In the pages of this book I share anecdotes and reflections from my time in and around the water. I also provide strategies and tools to support the transformation of our body, mind and spirit to help us, especially the gentle souls, move through life with more awareness, ease and joy.

Please note that while the word mermaid is, by its nature, gender specific, it is meant to be inclusive. Many humans relate to mermaid energy. It is my hope that if this book has come to you, it contains messages that support your soul's desire to dive deep into life in order to realise a common calling to love and to be loved.

*Tonia*

# Elements Of This Book

*"The psychotic drowns in the same waters in*

*which the mystic swims with delight."*

**— Joseph Campbell, Psychology of the Future**

Much like the sea itself, there is a rhythm to this book, which plays out in the elements described here. It is designed to be read in sequence, as there are some currents that flow from one chapter to another. That said, many of the chapters can float alone, so feel free to dive in where you wish!

## QUOTE

Each chapter starts with a quote to set the scene.

## SEA-ING YOUR LIFE DIFFERENTLY

This section offers suggestions for further research, action or exploration. Sea-ing your life differently can help you successfully jump on the next wave as well as than be left struggling in the surf. Sea-ing differently supports your development one wave at a time.

## CREST OF A WAVE

This section summarises the chapter and introduces the ideas that will follow in the next.

## MERMAID MINDSET

The mermaid mindset starts with a contradictory statement. By considering opposing concepts and working through the confusion often results in clarity of thought. The mermaid revels in the shifting sands and the changing currents. She is aware of the limitation of language to describe an all encompassing truth. Within the mermaid mindset you are encouraged to see the dichotomy in order to support a deeper engagement and consequential understanding of ideas.

## MERMAID MOTTOS

A mermaid motto is a fun way of describing an affirmation. Affirmations send vibrational messages to the Universe. They are written or spoken in the present tense. Some prefer to use an *"I am"* statement as it feels more uplifting and empowering for them to do so. For example:

*I am healthy.*

Some people feel uncomfortable with a mismatch between where they are now and where they hope to be, stated in the affirmation. This friction causes a challenge for the vibrational match that is being sought. To increase the feeling of truth behind the statement, using the words "I am willing" in front of what you hope for can reduce this friction. For example:

*I make the changes needed to support my optimum health.*

*I am willing to make the changes needed to support my optimum health.*

For others, saying the affirmation in a question form, a questfirmation, feels more in alignment. For example:

*Isn't it wonderful that I make changes to support my optimum health?*

Mermaid mottos are offered in each chapter and you are welcome to use, add, replace or alter them as appropriate.


## EXERCISE

Each chapter offers an exercise to deepen your engagement with the subject matter. It encourages you to explore more by putting an idea into practise.

## SEA-C

This section explores a word that encompasses a concept starting with the letter C (sea). There are many words that support contemplation at a deep level.

## A SPACE TO JOURNAL

Each chapter ends with a space to journal. I encourage you to spend time here. By journalling you can access and express your deep responses, as well as your initial reactions.

The first section provides a space to engage with the chapter in your own way. For example, you can make notes to remind yourself of relevant content. The second section poses questions for you to consider. Some questions will be easy to answer, whilst others will produce a mix of emotions. Before you consider the questions state the affirmation:

*I am willing to be open about the subject matter for my highest good.*

The last section provides a place to jot ideas down in response to two questions/statements. By recording these on your own personal action plan and signing it will encourage you to become more resolute in your commitment to take action. It is also an area to help you structure your priorities. Which of your possible choices will you action first?

# Prologue

## THE MERMAID RETURNS

*"Life is a sea of vibrant color. Jump in."*

*— A.D. Posey*

## THE GODDESS HAS LANDED

There's a new type of superstar dancing in our midst in ever-increasing numbers. Maybe you know one, you are one or you are metamorphosing into one. It's the energy of the yin as well as the yang, the belief in abundance rather than scarcity, of empowerment over control, the collective as opposed to the competitive, and love as opposed to fear.

We have seen these superstars in business; grounded and purposeful, manifesting with confidence. We have seen them socially; optimistic and positive, energetic and worshipped. We have seen them in families; sure and unshakeable, dependent and honoured.

The goddess has landed and many are taking her path.

I am in awe of her, revere her and aspire to her qualities, and yet I know that I can never truly encompass her, because the goddess is of the land. She is grounded on her Earth throne as comfortable with it as if it were her birthright, because indeed it is.

I love the glamour of the goddess, her sparkle, her presence and the embodiment of the divine feminine. I love her contribution and her energy, but still I know she is not me. I embody a different form. This form is as powerful, as feminine and with an equally vital role to play in the return of the divine feminine and the survival of our planet.

I know I am not alone. Many are hearing her call; it is the call of the mermaid.

## THE MERMAID RESURFACES

She's been here all along, swimming deep with grace and curiosity, watching and waiting for her time. Her message, her role and her love is as essential as her twin. For they are the yin and the yang, the goddess and the mermaid, and together they embrace the energy of the divine feminine.

A great deal is being written and shared about the goddess and now the mermaid joins her. There is no judgement in one over the other. Each plays her part in creating the whole, both essential to the balance needed for life and to soothe the drama of our world.

## THE MERMAID JOINS THE PARTY

The mermaid is more introverted, curious and playful than her goddess sister. She darts here and there, watching and waiting. She prefers invitations, and if she receives one she goes willingly and with all her heart. Mermaids are the empaths, the gentle souls with a memory of an ancient wisdom.

Mermaids arrive with an outward sparkle that reflects their inner shine and authentic spirit. They come in many forms, old and the young, for they are timeless, and as all timeless creatures, their true beauty is one of wisdom and heart, rather than ephemeral physical attributes. Theirs is the wisdom of all time that honours the strengths of both the land and the sea. Theirs is the message that invites you to dive deep to find your own hidden treasure and your eternal shine.

Once these magnificent creatures hid their beauty until they trusted it could be revealed, today they know there is no more time to waste. Mermaids are part of the sisterhood and they encourage reflection on who we really are for the sake of our happiness and our continued survival on our planet Earth.

# Chapter One

## LIFE AT THE SURFACE

*"I address you all tonight for who you truly are: wizards, mermaids, travelers, adventurers, and magicians. You are the true dreamers."*

**— Brian Selznick, *The Invention of Hugo Cabret***

## MERMAIDS AT THE SURFACE

**W**e all feel more at home in certain places and have a sense of discomfort in others. There is nothing inherently right or wrong about the place, but it is useful to explore the reason for this inner communication. Some of us fly high and enjoy the rush of falling through the air with a parachute, others feel the accomplishment of climbing mountains or following rivers to their natural source. Some prefer forests or meadows, whilst others find joy in the snow fields. Mermaids feel at home in the metaphoric waters, where life flows with an invigorating, constantly rejuvenating, refreshingly inclusive joy. Mermaids do not drown in the depth of life, but can feel stifled and ill at ease with life at the surface. This is why, if you feel the same, they suggest an inner dive so you can rediscover the treasures of life.

## HIGH AND DRY

- You think too much!
- You are too emotional!
- Why do you have to be different?
- Make your mind up!
- Why are you so quiet?
- You ask too many questions!
- Why do you need to be alone?
- Why do you need to know that?
- How did you know that?
- Slow down!
- Let your hair down; you can work on that tomorrow!
- Don't get all deep and meaningful with me!
- I don't understand you!

If these comments have been directed at you and you internalised them as criticisms, then you are likely to relate to my mermaid. To understand yourself and how you operate is incredibly liberating. To appreciate that there is nothing wrong with you does wonders for your self-esteem, how you live your life and respond to your world. I know I was doing internal cartwheels for weeks after discovering what it means to be an empath and an introvert and knowing that there are many individuals with the same traits.

This book invites you to look afresh at your life and your place within your world. This is the time to awaken and accept your strengths. Humanity needs you to accept yourself, to take action and to add to the ripple effect that is supporting the changing tide, honouring the harmonic rhythm once more. You were not meant to be left on the shores high and dry.

## STILL WATERS RUN DEEP

It was a perfect day. The sun was out, the air was cool and there was a sense of excitement on the boat. The water was calm and you couldn't really tell where it stopped and the sky began. As I looked far into the distance, where we had seen land only a few hours earlier, I realised any physical sign of it had vanished. It was as if the sea was happy to fill the whole planet with its turquoise blue. As I looked down onto the water, it moved slowly in one direction and then another, as if deliberately wanting my attention. It certainly had it. The sea spray caught the sunlight and rainbows bounced in front of my eyes as the boat gently rocked from side to side. As the rays of sunshine hit the water's surface they threw off glimmers of light, mesmerising like diamonds that captivate us with an eternal promise of love.

As I looked down, trying to see below the surface of the sea, I was sidetracked by the beauty of the colour. Subtle tones of turquoise mixed together and then parted, as if dancing partners on a stage of great importance. Although there was an expanse of space above me, right then it seemed as if the whole world was water and it was whispering to me, telling me of its depth and inviting me to jump in and explore once more.

Still waters run deep, and there is no longer the need to apologise for wanting a depth of knowledge or a thirst for deep conversation. There is no longer a need to apologise for the consequence of your nature or nurture because this world needs you all, the yin and the yang, the sky and the sea. When in harmony there is no conflict or power struggle. We exist together with our edges blurred.

## MAKING A SPLASH

We are all judged by others at one point or another, and some of us internalise this as our negative truth. We hold onto these judgments consciously or unconsciously, until they eventually feel like our own. You may not quite understand why you behave, respond or react as you do, or how this load is preventing you from moving forward easily in your life. This judgement, given by others and now interpreted as your truth, changes the lens through which you view your own experiences and believe is your reality.

This book invites you to dive into your life with a splash and to explore your experiences with depth and honesty. Using the mermaid as an insight tool and a catalyst for change, you can shake off your old tales and let the sparkle of your true self propel you forward with purpose and excitement, adding the shine needed in our world. It's my intention and hope that it will fast track you so you can claim your power and trust in your flow, rather than struggling with the current in order to please others. It is time to shake off the subtle cultural judgements you received for being on the empathic or introverted scale.

Dr. Christine Northrup, visionary pioneer and a leading authority in the field of women's health and wellness, describes a compass-sionate person as someone who can sympathise with the pain of another, whereas an empath, or what she refers to as an "old soul empath" actually feels the emotions. Some empaths find it hard to distinguish these emotions from their own. They know the truth of people because they feel the energy as if they *are* them. If someone is trying to be cheerful when they are really depressed, the empath will know. Empaths often want to make people feel better and are likely to disregard their own needs in order to console them. In her online course, *Dodging Energy Vampires,* Dr. Christine Northrup indicates that you may well be an empath if you relate to the following:

- Feel the emotions of others as if they are yours.
- Feel uncomfortable in the spotlight.
- Enjoy metaphysical topics, but often keep this quiet.
- Relate to being persecuted in many life times for what you knew.
- Are interested in conspiracy theories.
- Are driven to improve yourself.
- Have a tendency to hide your true nature for you have been rejected for your authenticity in the past.
- Dislike large noisy crowds.
- Are greatly disturbed by horror films or displays of great sadness or pain.

Living life as a sensitive soul in our modern world can be onerous. Other people's energy often leaves them feeling overwhelmed, confused and exhausted until they appreciate how to recharge and protect their own energy field. Empaths often feel betrayed, abandoned or shamed by their community, family or friends for behaving and responding differently from others, so they learn to hide their true nature to try to fit in and to be accepted. However, the wounds remain and influence their belief system, how they operate and their consequential life experiences.

An introvert can feel the same wounds as an empath and for similar reasons; it is a consequence of being different. However, whereas the empath feels judged for their intuitive knowing, the introvert feels judged for their need for space and time to recharge their energy alone. Answering a few key questions is a quick way to see whether you are on the introversion scale. The questions were compiled by Susan Cain, a former corporate lawyer and an introvert who in recent years has delved deeper into the study of human nature, with a focus on highlighting the many strengths of introversion. The following was taken from her Psychology Today post entitled, *QUIZ: Are You an Introvert or an Extrovert? (And Why It Matters) The north and south of temperament.* The more you agree with, the more likely you are to be an introvert:

- I prefer one-on-one conversations to group activities.
- I enjoy solitude.
- I dislike conflict.
- I dislike small talk, but I enjoy talking in-depth about topics that matter to me.
- If I had to choose, I'd prefer a weekend with absolutely nothing to do to one with too many things scheduled.
- I feel drained after being out and about, even if I've enjoyed myself.
- I like to celebrate birthdays on a small scale, with only one or two close friends or family members.
- I'm not a big risk-taker.
- In classroom situations, I prefer lectures to seminars.

What happens when the qualities and temperament of an empath and introvert collide and merge? You discover my mermaid in all her glory, swimming and playing in the waves. She feels the joy of life because she has dived deep into her shadow, healed her wounds and accepted her light.

After engaging in self-development for some time, I found my missing piece that supported my understanding of key concepts and my ability to respond and integrate ideas appropriately. My mermaid is my missing piece and encompasses all the pieces. By understanding life experiences through her eyes, the issues experienced by both the empath and the introvert are appreciated and valued, giving permission once more for their true nature to resurface and to splash onto the world's stage.

## ON AN EVEN KEEL

As the boat slowed down and anchored, everyone was eager and ready for the exploration of a new dive site. The sun was beaming a blanket of warmth over us and we were excited to enter the water for relief. There was a flurry of chatter and activity by the majority of the group as they prepared for that first plunge. I was looking over the side, staring intently at the water. It wasn't long before a few people noticed this and came over to discover the cause of such focus. Perceiving nothing of significance, they began asking, "What are you doing?" and "What can you see?" Disconnecting from my thoughts, I turned round and replied, "Nothing, I was just thinking!"

"Oh, you think too much!" they retorted, looking slightly exasperated. I paused for a beat as if wondering whether to reply, but they had already walked away, their attention diverted by a different source. As I started to pull on my wetsuit, I smiled to myself at a joke I could hear being told on the other side of the boat. I smiled again when I realised I didn't think *too* much, I just didn't talk *so* much. That left time and space for my mind to receive informational downloads. A girl I didn't know that well came over and asked, "What do you sense?" I looked at her and winked. "We'll see dolphins today. Lots of them!"

Finally, the group was ready. We all entered the water with anticipation. We were not disappointed. A pod of dolphins greeted us before speeding off into the blue yonder.

I hope that in sharing some experiences and insights I gained through diving, I will help you better acknowledge and come to appreciate who you are. It is by diving deep and seeing yourself from a different perspective that you gain your confidence, move with your flow and find your joy and place within the world. The story above is one of many incidents that I could offer about the joy of slowing down and tuning in. Something special occurs when you take time to go within, as well as responding to the world around you.

## A MIXTURE OF MERMAIDS

The mermaid in this book sparkles from the inside out and from the outside in. She has a tale to tell about the importance of claiming your shine and your place in the sisterhood. She dances between metaphoric, symbolic, literal and archetypical, knowing that she cannot really be defined. Sometimes my mermaid may swim beside you, be you or me, as well as being an esoteric energy.

My mermaid is elusive. She moves between worlds and swims playfully between concepts. Her mission to help us reclaim the power of our soul is easier to define than the form she chooses to ensure its realisation. Some definitions will be explored in this chapter and developed in the next, but for now we can see the mermaid as a tool for self-exploration and insight. She is best matched for those on the introverted scale, with an empathic heart who hear the call for change by the divine feminine. I will switch unapologetically between my definitions to support her message. As an introverted and empathic writer, I have no issue with this approach and I hope that as an introverted and empathic reader you will delight in it.

If you picked this book to read, I hope you already feel the connection. To help you become clearer still, consider how many of the following words resonate with you as something you have, yearn for or need to overcome. If they resonate, there is a strong chance you are part of the mermaid sisterhood, especially if you also have the desire to swim under the stars and ride the waves of life. Here are some of the mermaids' attributes and characteristics:

- Esoteric
- Empathic
- Inner calling
- Freedom
- Introverted
- Synchronistic
- Playful
- Idiosyncratic
- Peaceful
- Curious
- Intuitive
- Mysterious

## THE METAPHORIC MERMAID

The mermaid is a wonderful metaphor for this deep dive into your inner world. It also aids your understanding of what can sometimes be contrasting, conflicting and confusing concepts. It is by understanding and accepting the contradictions of life that you can surf the waves and allow the universal tides to surprise you. Labels are here to help, temporarily. Many can be used simultaneously. Sometimes the definitions are an exaggerated version of what you may be experiencing; nevertheless, presenting them in such a way can assist your understanding of who you are, where you want to be and what is preventing you from achieving this and hence, motivate you into action. The mermaid integrates the characteristics of an empath and an introvert beautifully and is a wonderful balance to her extroverted sister, the goddess.

Mermaids are a wonderful barrier, softening the need to talk directly about yourself. There is a protection in this, as introverts and empaths don't like the limelight and are seldom comfortable baring their souls. Using this analogy is a less intimidating introspective tool by which you can share and analyse the mermaid's attributes and how they may apply to you or you to them.

Any understanding of the metaphoric mermaid would not be complete without referencing the work of Carl Jung and his students, specifically around the iceberg metaphor. To summarise their explanation, your conscious awareness is like the tip of an iceberg. It is above the water and in your realm of awareness. It can be seen, described and it is where most of us dwell. There is much more beneath the surface; it is beyond your initial awareness, but it is accessible if you dive down. If you are willing to explore this you can gain a greater understanding of yourself. It is within this part of your psyche that you can rediscover repressed memories and traumas, including those from childhood that you locked away because you didn't have the skills to process them adequately at the time.

If a third of your psyche is above the water and your repressed memories are another third below, the iceberg goes deeper still, into the realms of the esoteric. It is here you are connected to humanity, time and space. It is in this part the introverted empath dwells, or at least senses.

In order to successfully navigate around an iceberg, the whole of it needs to be considered, not just what is visible above the surface. The same is true for you. As you navigate your life on land and action the laws of manifestation, you benefit from understanding the totality of your psyche. Every part of yourself yearns to be integrated, accepted and acknowledged.

## THE MERMAID ARCHETYPE

The sun was high in the sky with only a solitary white cloud distracting viewers from an otherwise pure blue canvas. There was a breeze created by the motion of the boat and the sun's rays felt like kisses from above. From the smiles around I could tell, for that moment, all was well for those with me. The surface of the water looked like a stage carefully designed for maximum impression. This stunning stage wasn't wasted, for suddenly to our delight a dolphin breached in front of us, scattering diamond-like sparkles high into the air. As we watched, more dolphins joined this impromptu spectacle and our awestruck team watched in wonder.

I contrasted my experience of that perfect day with the reality of many of the sailors of old, battling the seas day and night, in all weathers and all seasons. The strength of character, the sturdiness of the body needed to survive such experiences seemed almost unfathomable. I recalled that blue as a colour was a more recent label and that the sailors used to call the sea black. There have been instances where I could understand why. I reflected on how many people lost their lives and the age old tales of mermaids. It is interesting that even in times of such harshness and pending doom there is still a desire to believe in a glimmer of hope, that something beautiful is there for us when everything we once knew is being taken away.

As I watched the dolphins play, I imagined the mermaids dancing with them, just out of sight. It would be just like them to incite such a marvellous display and yet, take no credit. For the mermaid does not need to be centre stage, adorned with jewels and lights. Her pleasure is giving to others and providing the space for them to shine by healing one hurt heart at a time.

The mermaid is not only a metaphor, but also an archetype, anchored in the global and collective unconsciousness. Although I learnt much about archetypes through the writings of Carl Jung, I had not fully appreciated their importance in our day to day lives until I became familiar with the work of Caroline Myss, Denise Duffield-Thomas, Kendall SummerHawk and Marianne Williamson. Their interpretation and application of archetypes – namely that we could describe characteristics that could apply to a number of people and therefore, support their healing – was fascinating to me. Through the mermaid we gain a glimpse of society's universal and eternal themes, including our instinct and our desire to be whole in both a personal and global sense. Many introverted empaths feel this, even if they haven't had a way of describing it.

The archetypal mermaid in her healthy expression is joyful and playful, sensual and confident, creative and nurturing as well as abundant and mysterious. In her unhealthy expression she represents the hurt inner child, the fractionalised soul and the drowning and out of control psyche.

## SOUL SISTER

Once the awareness of the mermaid's message is appreciated and actioned the label can be released and the mermaid can happily swim away. You do not need to own the label, for to define yourself forever would restrict and limit you. You just need to swim with it for a while to understand more about how you process yourself and your world. Remember, the mermaids are here to liberate us. Their message is about diving deep. It is about understanding our contradictions and challenges in order to support our inner peace and the realisation of our collective soul contract. The mermaid offers a compass to help us action our inner calling that never seems to relent, urging us to play our part in supporting others, and by doing so takes our own life in new and exciting directions.

We all have an element of the mermaid energy. For some it is prevalent and overriding, for others it is hidden or denied. We can learn from each side.

I hope this book helps you, my introverted sister with a soul connection, to make shifts in your life, one wave at a time. This way you can go with your flow and not against it. You can feel worthy of being part of the sisterhood, encompassing the power of the divine feminine and shining your light into the darkness.

*"Some say there are no such things as mermaids. I say they just haven't dived deep enough!" teased the mermaid!*

## SEA-ING YOUR LIFE DIFFERENTLY

Developing new awareness can support significant change. This starts one wave at a time. Learn more about the traits of introversion:

- Research websites that celebrate famous introverts and the contributions they make.

- Appreciate that successful introverts use their traits as their source of strength.

- Join groups such as Facebook, that celebrate introversion through uplifting and humorous posts.

- Have fun guessing where on the scale your family and friends might be and consider if understanding this can support more grace and ease in the relationships.

## CREST OF A WAVE

Life at the surface can be beautiful. Many function well on this level and enjoy the experience. Alternatively, you may be aware of a calling that there is more to life than your five senses indicate and your present experience suggests. You feel the pull to dive deep, however hard you have previously tried to ignore such sensations.

This chapter introduced the mermaid as a tool for self-exploration and, ultimately, self-realisation. In the following chapters, with the help of the mermaids, you will dive deep into a range of topics to bring greater understanding of what it means to be on planet Earth as an empathic introvert.

## MERMAID MINDSET

*I am the same as you for we are one, but we are totally unique with our own roles to play.*

Feeling secure with your understanding of contradictions is a powerful gift. Claim it and feel the liberation and comfort it brings.

Many empaths and introverts live in dichotomy and have felt judged by those who don't understand its value. Now, instead of it being a challenge it is a reason for your shine. Others may not understand you, but it is important only for you to understand yourself. You dance effortlessly between viewpoints, knowing the truth each holds. In time, the true value of this will be more widely acknowledged.

## MERMAID MOTTOS

Before you journal, reflect on some mermaid mottos to support your ongoing willingness to dive into yourself and your motivation to take the necessary action as a consequence. You are welcome to jump into mine.

*I dive deep within myself and happily acknowledge the message of the mermaid.*

*It is fabulous to gain insights that support my higher good.*

*I eagerly engage in the journal pages and undertake the exercises with honesty.*

## EXERCISE

AFFIRMATIONS

There is a tendency for the mermaid to put herself down, to underplay her value and to dull her shine. This exercise asks you to be kind to yourself and to celebrate your good points as if you were talking about a best friend. No one needs to see what you write, so don't hold back. Write everything you would like to have noticed in positive affirmations or "I am" statements. Allow your kindness and compassion for others to shine for yourself. Recognise and appreciate the many qualities and strengths you have. For example:

*I am thoughtful.*

*I am kind.*

Have fun with this. In addition, write down the introversion and empathic traits you see in yourself and turn them into positive affirmations. For example:

*I embrace my shyness and continue to develop my confidence.*

*I value my time alone and honour the benefit this gives me and my ability to serve others.*

*I enjoy being curious about the world and sharing different viewpoints with my friends.*

## SEA-C

CONTEMPLATE

To contemplate creates opportunities for greater understanding and to see in a different way. To contemplate is to live in the expansive

Universe of possibilities, before you narrow them down into a temporary reality.

*I contemplate many things, sometimes for answers and sometimes just to be open to unexpected realisations.*

*When I take time to contemplate life I find hidden treasures.*

# CHAPTER ONE: LIFE AT THE SURFACE

*A space to journal my thoughts from this chapter…*

_____

_____

_____

_____

_____

_____

_____

_____

_____

_____

_____

_____

_____

_____

_____

_____

_____

_____

_____

_____

_____

_____

# A CONSIDERATION

What do I enjoy about life at the surface?

_____

_____

What areas could be improved?

_____

_____

Do I sense a calling and do I acknowledge this?

_____

_____

Do I take enough time to reflect and engage?

_____

_____

What attributes of the mermaid do I have?

_____

_____

# COMMITMENT AND MY PLAN OF ACTION

Today I will commit to learning more about empaths and introverts to develop my understanding.

_____

_____

_____

What is my plan of action to develop my understanding of my own empathic and introversion traits, which I have felt hold me back, but would now like to start valuing as gifts? (Create a to-do list to remind yourself, adding the date/time you will engage. For example, "When will I study? When will I self-reflect? When will I notice my empathic or introverted nature in action?")

_____

_____

_____

_____

_____

_____

_____

_____

_____

_____

_____

_I commit. Signed:_ _____

# Chapter Two

## DIVING DEEP

*"In a sea of human beings, it is difficult, at times even*

*impossible, to see the human as being."*

**— Aysha Taryam**

## MERMAIDS DIVE DEEP

Quiet by nature and a need to rejuvenate alone, it is easy to see how mermaids can be misunderstood by their more gregarious sisters. A mermaid's introverted and empathic nature means she doesn't want to party with the crowd, but this doesn't mean she is comfortable with isolation nor that she has shunned the group. However, as she doesn't follow allocated leaders, she can often be misunderstood and it is she who is ultimately not included in the group and feels like she's on the outside looking in. With time, the mermaid may choose to dive deep, to hear an inner calling that tells her she is connected to all things and there is no need for separation. Diving deep is a perfect way to find your way back home.

## A METAPHORIC CROWN

They flew by with grace and ease, like celestial beings, turning effortlessly to revisit us once more. These were majestic creatures, comfortable with their power and appearing connected to their source. Manta rays still mesmerise however many times I see them. I had been told they are the most intelligent fish in the sea, due to the size of their brain and their ability to communicate through a complex system that allows these creatures to be closely in tune with each other. When relaxed their lobes are open, allowing divers to come a little closer; if the lobes are closed a diver would be wise to keep a distance or the manta rays might dart away. As the manta rays swam, or symbolically flew by, it was as if the whole sea was their space to be. I could visualise their metaphoric crown and sensed they owned their power with pride and humility. I was star struck.

## STAR STRUCK

There's a whisper from the sisterhood about the resurgence of something brilliant. There is another kind of energy being acknowledged, a phenomena resurfacing to help shine a light in the world. This energy is part of the sea and part of the land, part human and also spirit. She sparkles as she carries within her jewels and sacred gifts.

The mermaid is perfectly aligned in her mission with her sisters on land, even if they have been distant for some time. The goddess may laugh at their differences, but she believes in their common aim and has reverence for their shared love. The goddess hears the mermaid's song, entrusted with the mission to manifest a majestic way for our age. The mermaids and the goddesses set aside their polarity and come together with compassion for the greater good. The goddess is grounded, confident in her domain and brings with her order and instruction. The goddess expects the return of the divine feminine and love on Earth. She insists on justice and fairness and knows there is a better way for the world to be. The mermaid dives here and there, listening, whispering, serving and suggesting. She is part of the vibe. She feels the connectivity of the sisterhood and has felt the dreams of us all. She is essential to the integration of understanding because she is the balance and she is here to nurture and heal our souls.

Maybe we have always needed heroes, the legends, the icons and the myths to keep us inspired. The stories of lost underwater cities of ancient worlds, mythology, folklore and fairy tales, spell books, unicorns and magic lamps continue to fascinate. Maybe we need to feel star struck because we no longer acknowledge our own light.

## TAKING THE PLUNGE

The sea is an incredible place with something for everyone. Some people enjoy walking by it, sailing on it or swimming in it. Far fewer are as passionate about being under its surface, but there's an amazing world below waiting to dazzle you if you're willing to take the plunge.

Although it is still a minority sport, more and more people are diving. Many become quickly enthralled, whether their experience began with conscious intention or a seemingly random invitation. Others remain fearful of entering the sea for a paddle, let alone swimming underwater. I have always felt comfortable in water; however, diving deep required some deep inner work, and the two seemed paradoxically intertwined. As one set of experiences were eased into my area of acceptance, another would surface, coaxing me to explore deeper still. With each submergence there was a transmutation, a cleansing and a liberation of the soul. It was through these experiences that the mermaid came into my existence.

In my first book, *Spiritual Seas: Diving into Life,* I noted with irony and humour that I, a self-declared child of the stars, found myself not soaring up into space with aliens from other planets, but diving deep with marine life that at times appear extraterrestrial. I did not glide through space in a space suit, but floated along in a wetsuit. Taking the plunge into the sea and having the chance to be wrapped lovingly in the water's warm embrace, I felt at home. The experiences I have had and the marine life I've seen have been incredible and I am thankful for every encounter.

The early days were not always easy. There were challenges. There were techniques I had to learn, skills to master and a mindset I needed to encourage. Whilst diving you have a responsibility for yourself and for your buddy, not just in terms of safety, but in honouring the quality of the dive experience. Panicking underwater presents a real danger on both counts. Using up your air by rapid breathing shortens the dive. When you are in a fear mode your air consumption is high. Under the water you need to react and respond swiftly. You need to master your thoughts, control your emotions and slow down a pounding heart if the dive is to be enjoyable and last for an appropriate length of time. Through diving deep I had the chance to confront many fears. It amplified my awareness of what I was thinking and feeling. My fears ranged from not having enough air, not trusting my equipment, worrying about the currents or thinking that I would become a tasty morsel for a hungry fish.

In the beginning I was obsessed with my air gauge. I would watch the pointer move towards the redline of fifty bar and as it got closer I felt myself draw deeper and faster. As I got more comfortable with diving and also more aware of my thoughts and feelings, I was able to regulate these and my breathing rate slowed down. My air consumption hardly goes below a hundred bar now. Under the water I had the opportunity to witness firsthand the almost instant link between my thoughts and the outer consequence on my air consumption. The implications of this in other areas of my life were profound.

There are two main reasons we dive deep into our inner world - deliberately, through a hobby, yoga practice or heart-to-heart with a friend, or due to an unexpected life event such as a medical emergency or loss of a relationship. I had the opportunity to dive deep when I was introduced to the work of Louise Hay, a motivational speaker and the founder of Hay House Publishing. I also discovered her many amazing Hay House authors, a roster that includes Wayne Dyer, Caroline Myss and Bruce Lipton, to name a few. I attended spiritual workshops, completed courses and immersed myself in as much as I could through internet searches and visiting websites. In addition to Heal Your Life®, I became certified in Neuro-Linguistic Programming, Basic Counselling, Reiki, Quantum-Touch, Spiritual Life Coaching, Colour Therapy, Oracle Card Reading, Sacred Money Archetypes, Facial Reflexology and Ho'oponopono, to name a few. It was during this time that I also clocked over four hundred and fifty dives. Through these explorations I began to appreciate the connection between the inner world and the outer world, personal responsibility and choice.

Through this immersion I became happier swimming with the contradictions of life, more comfortable with the shifting of sands and crashing of the waves, for I swam with mermaids. I now trust that miracles come out of the blue and I am more prepared to go with the flow of synchronistic events rather than fight the currents of change. I have more tools and strategies to keep me afloat and maintain a peace of mind for longer durations. I have released my heavy load and have witnessed a ripple effect across the waters.

As with the sea, once you go below the surface and start to explore, you discover a whole new world. If you are prepared to take the plunge life is never the same again.

## THE MERMAID'S WAY

Whilst on a boat waiting for a dive, I was observing the still and peaceful sky when a sudden commotion disturbed the calm. A series of pilots were practising for a show, zooming their planes through the air with precision, demonstrating their skills. They were fast and furious, and very loud. Their mastery was undeniable and captured the attention of everyone on the boat. Just watching them I felt the adrenaline coursing through my body, for they appeared seconds away from potential disaster. I imagined the pilots and then their loved ones watching from a distance. The noise was so intense that nothing else could continue until they had passed, leaving huge trails in the sky to prove that they had been there.

That day there had been a similar commotion under the water, slower and gentler, but just as impressive and as captivating as the planes in the sky. There had been a sighting of a whale shark. It had moved with grace and silence and once gone there was no sign that it had ever been present. So it is with mermaids. They are quiet and gentle; they do not need to be seen. They communicate in different ways, offering a message of hope for humanity. They are here to show us another way and in the midst of chaos they offer peace.

Do you sense them? Are you also attracted to the mermaid's way?

- Do you enjoy the beauty of the world in a profound way?

- Do you have an infinity with quiet places?

- Are you guided to develop your soulfulness?

- Do you have a strong sense of justice?

- Do you get excited by oxymorons?

- Are you drawn to learn about sacred missions?

- Do you feel guided to learn more about ancient wisdoms?

- Are there times you question whether Earth is your soul home?

- Do you like to leave things better or at least as you found them.

- Do you find speaking a limited form of communication?

- Do you get frustrated by the mechanics of your body?

- Do you feel linear time is an illusion?

- Do you receive informational downloads?

- Do you think conceptually rather than linearly?

- Are you misunderstood by some people, but totally fascinate others?

- Are you guided to support a cause?

- Do you relish deep talk and lose interest in shallow conversations?

If you resonate with these you'd benefit from a trip to the beach!

## TO THE BEACH

The turtles crawl from their hatching place to the sea. They are vulnerable to predators during this journey, but there is no other way.

It is programmed in their DNA. Knowing that this journey is necessary does not make it any less heart rending to watch. Many will not make it, but for those who do the journey is worth it. The water is their home and salvation.

What are your hopes and dreams, and what is holding you back? What is your default mode of behaviour? Feeling stuck on the sandbanks when the sea is calling is an uncomfortable place to be.

Many mermaids do not feel completely at home on the land, as they feel encumbered by the human body, limited by the need for speech and trapped by the rigidity of the physical world. Introverted and spiritually guided with a strong sense of purpose, they can feel ungrounded when that purpose seems impossible to achieve. They feel like outliers on this plane. The mermaid has her shadow side and when she is there, it is dark. This is when a deep dive is especially useful.

Some mermaids turn to books in their search for answers; yet, often they don't connect with the language or the sentiment. Authors are not always appreciative of the mermaids' traits and spiritual aspects, and a generic approach can push buttons in a way that is not engaging or empowering. In fact, it may send the mermaids swimming off into the blue yonder at top speed, finding the nearest shell in which to hide. Mermaids are not motivated the way many others are; they need their own language and strategies that are more suitable for their empathic and introverted nature. In other words, one size fits all self-help books are not the most effective way of encouraging change. Fortunately, there is a growing number of books offering invaluable information and support for gentle souls, such as Dr. Judith Orloff's *The Empath's Survival* Guide. This book is full of ideas for those who want to nurture their empathy and intuition and develop coping skills for living in a high-stimulus world.

Mermaids have a contribution to make, therefore it is important that they find the tools to heal and empower themselves. Understanding how they are wired is a good start for both mermaids and self-help writers alike. Mermaids can have an issue around their visibility and also the validity of their message. This in turn impacts their sense of validation, the level of their vibration and overall self-esteem. They respond better with a gentle, blurred-edged approach to change, one that allows a whole lot of privacy, where personal space, including the mind, is considered sacred.

## VULNERABLE MERMAIDS

A jackfish went by with its serious, downturned mouth. It appeared as if it were carrying the world's problems on its gills. Then a school of grey fish darted past in tight succession, all but one that lingered back. I saw another school of fish, again seemingly all the same, but on second glance, one fish was different. There is always one.

Even though data suggests that a third to half of the population is on the introversion scale and about fifteen to twenty percent are highly sensitive people, it can feel like you are the odd one out in a society that overflows with noise and activity. The loud enthusiasm, the spontaneous group activities and the general confident chit-chat and hustling for the limelight can make it hard to fit in when your whole being is shouting, "I don't belong here; let me out!" Preferring smaller groups, more intimate discussions and less frivolity, those with the mermaid energy can feel out of sync in crowds. They can interpret this as meaning there is something wrong with them.

My discomfort at being in the spotlight resulted in me missing out on my graduation. It was the same at my wedding. The thought of being the centre of attention filled me with dread. I still needed and appreciated validation and so the certificate in my hand and the pat on the back in a quiet celebratory occasion meant everything to me. As did my wedding, witnessed by close friends that helped make it a memorable, and a mermaid-friendly, occasion.

Mermaids do not relish small talk. They live in the question or at least expect their present opinions to change. They don't like to be pinned down with questions that imply a cut and dried answer. They enjoy a few moments to consider their response, which is not always possible in the fast-paced back and forth of many social interactions. Like a scientist challenging a hypothesis, a mermaid lives in the ever-evolving reality, as elusive as the shining stars to a child who tries to understand how they can already be dead at the time of seeing.

Mermaids, when they shine, are entertaining and as good a company as you would hope to have. But in the back of their mind there is usually a lingering voice, "I may want to go soon. How can I slink off?" It makes social gatherings challenging, especially if they have to be there or they worry about offending others. Introverts get their energy and recharge their energy by being on their own, as opposed to extroverts who get their energy from being with others. Added to this, the mermaid's sensitivities means she also picks up on the nuances around her and is deeply affected by the vibration of others. This can get overwhelming in larger groups.

It is not always obvious to recognise a mermaid at work or at play. They have learnt strategies to look as if they fit into a world where they perceive they don't belong. They take the stage by preparation, hiding behind a character or because they passionately believe in their message more than their discomfort. Although they do it admirably, being with others takes its toll on their energy levels. Some have created niches, such as using the internet where they contribute within stronger barriers. They can use social media where videoing from the sanctuary of their home feels safer, but can have the reach of millions.

Walking into a party alone or opening a closed door have both been challenging experiences for me in the past, causing emotional turmoil out of proportion to the event. Equally, I love self-development, but not if there is an expectation for me to participate in front of others. For a long time I thought this was a character flaw. Now, with my knowledge of the traits of an empath and an introvert, I understand myself better. I have choices. I can let my traits hinder me, leaving me vulnerable, or I can work with them. Like a fair-skinned individual who knows they burn in the sunshine, there are options, compromises and short term solutions. One can wear protective clothing or limit the amount of exposure to direct sunshine, or stay out of the sun altogether and enjoy inside activities. When you know yourself you can choose to be defined and contained by your traits or use them as the springboard to new heights.

## VIBRANT MERMAIDS

The mermaid's message is not that we do everything perfectly. Rather it is to enjoy who we are and what we do. Part of our experience is to engage with the unexpected and to feel the range of emotions that result from our trials and tribulations. What the mermaid encourages is for us to learn from our experiences, our reactions and our emotions. Find the lesson of humility and find a way to see the light. Don't always take other people's judgements too seriously, but instead find the grace in knowing they are not a reflection of you, but of them. Be willing to forgive in a world where we all, at times, are just trying to stay afloat. We have a choice to action the mermaid's message or leave it for another time.

*"Some people say jump and I say how deep?"*
*laughed the mermaid.*

## SEA-ING YOUR LIFE DIFFERENTLY

Acquiring knowledge is empowering and creates channels for change. Change is coming. You can feel it. Your choice is when to dive and how deep? Consider the following:

- Explore the concept of archetypes as a vehicle for diving deep without it feeling as personal as a direct enquiry.

- Learn about the different archetypes and how they play out in your life. Some may be relevant whilst others merely for interest. Knowledge interlinks eventually.

- Research more about affirmations, the "I am" statement and visualisation, and how these alter your point of attraction.

## CREST OF A WAVE

When you understand yourself better and appreciate that there is nothing wrong with who you are, it is easier to rid yourself of the tales you tell yourself that prevent your flow. You are better positioned to reclaim your power and to ride your waves with joy. This chapter explored the characteristics of the mermaid and encouraged you to dive deep in order to soothe your soul and the collective soul of us all. It is your time to shine.

In chapter three you will discover that you can gain a greater understanding of yourself through the tool of reflection. Through this tool you can shift your old stories into ones that move your life forward with more ease.

## MERMAID MINDSET

*I remind you of the past so you can be in the present.*

Interactions with others and ourselves can cause confusion and challenges when you respond from an automatic programming that you are unaware of. Life provides you with opportunities and signposts that invite you to dive deep into yourself so you can resurface with more compassion and a greater understanding of who you are.

It was through my thirst to understand my world better that I swam with my mermaid. She helped me appreciate why some of the advice I received resonated whilst other advice pushed me further astray. I began to acknowledge and live in the light of my gentle soul rather than to live within the shadow.

## MERMAID MOTTOS

Before you journal, reflect on some mermaid mottos to encourage your ongoing willingness to dive deep. You are welcome to use mine to get you started.

*I explore my inner world and find treasures that support my development.*

*It is liberating to reframe judgement into praise.*

*I happily engage in the journal pages.*

## EXERCISE

### VISUALISATION

As with affirmations, visualisation is another way of altering your present vibration. You often visualise the future in the negative, unaware that you are adding to the potential for its realisation. Why not play with visualising good outcomes consciously? For instance, if you are heading to meet some new people and hear yourself saying, "They won't like me!" try consciously replacing it with a statement such as, "I have a lovely time!" or "We have a great time together!" and visualise that good time. Sense the merriment and hear the laughter. See what transpires with a more positive approach.

## SEA-C

## COMPASSION

When you are willing to notice, in a gentle way, where you could be misguided or out of alignment with your truth, you open up a space for another possibility. Develop your willingness for compassion as you would a muscle for strength, through practice. Be open to a more generous way of thinking when you feel yourself in judgement. Allow negativity to disperse as you judge yourself and others less. Become aware that by doing so you release tension that seemed locked in place. This will allow you to feel lighter. With compassion, rather than judgement, resistance lessens and the process of change becomes easier.

*As I read I will be open to the possibility of discovering something that is holding me back from experiencing the life I desire.*

*As I read, I will consider what I could alter about my present thoughts and actions that could be shift-tudinal.*

# CHAPTER TWO: DIVING DEEP

*A space to journal my thoughts from this chapter…*

_____

_____

_____

_____

_____

_____

_____

_____

_____

_____

_____

_____

_____

_____

_____

_____

_____

_____

_____

_____

_____

_____

# A CONSIDERATION

How deep are you willing to dive for a better life experience?

_____

_____

_____

How big a splash are you unashamedly and playfully prepared to make in this life?

_____

_____

_____

What holds you back from making a big splash?

_____

_____

_____

What encouragement would help you take the plunge?

_____

_____

_____

# COMMITMENT AND MY PLAN OF ACTION

Today I commit to noticing my thoughts of judgement and allow compassionate thoughts to disperse them.

_____

_____

_____

What is my plan of action for engaging in the exercises and strategies that resonate for me in this book? Keep adding ideas to an ongoing list. For example, "When will I start to play with visualisation? Could I try it right now?"

_____

_____

_____

_____

_____

_____

_____

_____

_____

_____

_____

_____

*I commit. Signed:* _____

# Chapter Three

## REFLECTIONS

*"Love is like the sea. The waves of life, they ebb and flow; they come and go. Time sweeps us away from each other. Love always brings us back."*

— **Kate McGahan**

## THE MERMAID'S REFLECTION

There are many opportunities in life through which we can learn, develop and change. Interactive workshops, for example, are gaining momentum and popularity. For many mermaids, however, self-development is more insightful during quieter moments. They prefer online courses, books and methods where they can ensure a level of privacy and where they don't need to share or chant with a crowd. They prefer a gentler environment where they feel safe. Mermaids have revelations, but not on demand. The vibes from other people can confuse and overwhelm their sensitive system.

For the mermaid, an alternative way of gaining clarity is through the tool of reflection. Such reflection is threefold: your inner world reflecting back your outer experience; a sign you find in your environment that reflects back an insight in response to a request you consciously or unconsciously made; and a time of inward calm that results in surprising revelations. A mermaid's challenge is to appreciate the value of such reflections and then to consider how best to access and action the messages they offer.

## SEA-ING THE LIGHT

The moon appeared centre stage in the night sky as we observed it from the top deck of the boat. It was beautiful and mysterious, keeping the memories of the day and the promise of tomorrow. It reflected onto the water, creating a path of white on the sea's surface as it spread light into the darkness. As captivating as it was, there were fluorescent beams gaining our attention elsewhere.

At the back of the boat the lights were on and hundreds of tiny exuberant fish were jumping high into the air. Their joy was short-lived as they found themselves upside down on the deck and flapping furiously for any chance of falling back into the sea. What instinct made these fish fly, kamikaze-style, onto the boat deck? Deep down are we all programmed to return to the light?

## MERMAIDS MATTER

Mermaids matter because they are the balance. They are the reminder of other possibilities and the invitation for us to look beyond what the eyes see, to a place where we can feel a soul connection. Mermaids encourage us to see and feel the invisible, hear the unspoken, believe in miracles and acknowledge the eternal energy that links us all. They call us to swim together and feel comfortable in the paradox of our existence. The mermaids urge us to excel in our humanity.

When in balance the mermaid owns her power, using the energy of the yin and yang appropriately. She harnesses the power of the currents and flows with ease with the tides of change. She encompasses mystery and demonstrates mastery, both entwined and intrinsically linked with the ebb and flow of life. She sees the periphery as well as a central focus, the larger picture within the smallness of the drama. When in her flow, the mermaid reveals clarity and beauty in the midst of chaos, hope in the midst of disaster and light during the darkest of moments.

There are differing definitions for yin and yang just as there are various artworks to represent them. In general terms they are two opposing, but interconnected energies contained within the cosmic force. Symbolically, this combined energy is represented by a circle with the yin feminine energy making up half of the circle in black and the yang masculine energy filling the other half in white. Each section contains a dot of the other. When this force divides in two - the yin and yang, each with its own specific qualities - it creates physical matter in the world.

Mermaids that have claimed their light have the confidence to let their shine sparkle into the world and are making an incredible impact. They are part of the renewed energy on the stage of life, urging us to reflect on how we do business, educate and nurture our young, how we approach politics, relationships and how to honour humanity. There is a change afloat and with each ignited soul, the ripple effect becomes stronger and more encompassing.

Mermaids have a dream; a song to share with the world. Sadly, some mermaids still struggle in their shadow side. It is easy to appreciate why they don't share their song, but retreat to the safety of a shell. Introverted by nature and previously judged for it, coupled with a sensitive soul and a universal memory of ancestral pain, they often have a belief system that no longer serves them. Their low self-esteem causes them to shut down their dreams and mute their voices as a protective response. They can feel overwhelmed by the magnitude of what is needed on Earth and the role they are required to play. They are confused by the laws of the land.

What is useful for the mermaid, with her empathic and introverted disposition, is to understand how this land works and her place on it. Then she can use her emotions as a compass, her outer experience as a map and a reflection of her inner beliefs, and her intuition as the designer's creative hand. She can flow in harmony with the rhythm of life whilst simultaneously singing her song.

## WAVES OF EXISTENCE

Mermaids are energetic by nature and hence fast-flowing. This is why the sea is such a perfect conduit for them. On land, however, some can appear anxious, impatient and nervous. Finding time to quieten the mind and the nervous system to develop an inner peace, whether through walking or meditation, is extremely beneficial. The mermaid on land does well to cultivate such a state in order to see and feel the messages available in everyday situations. During such times they allow a larger realm of possibilities to come together, offering clarity on which way to flow.

A mermaid will also find it useful to appreciate what wave of energy she is operating from or in. There are times she will flow in a state of yin, the feminine receptive energy. Here she moves with ease and grace and as one with her environment. There is no friction as she rides the waves with joy. This is a time for her to accept, to receive and to enjoy the synchronicity of life. At times it seems that things materialise before they are even imagined. This occurs as she is in alignment with her true self and has conscious awareness of her beliefs and thoughts, which serve her well. Before this occurs, the mermaid would have been in the masculine yang energy. She had decided to ride a different wave which required the need to cross a current flow. This would have involved planning, organising and action to make it possible. The mermaid is comfortable with both energies.

The issues arise when a mermaid becomes stuck within one energy. If over-dominant in her yin she may find herself being swept along a current and in a direction she doesn't want to go, or feel exhausted as she tries to defy the tides in her over-reliance in the yang. The mermaid benefits from exploring and understanding the power and potential of both and how to reside and flow in and between them. As you dive deeper into such understanding you appreciate that the world you reside in is also subjected to the same energy vortexes and you can use this knowledge to assist you in your decision-making process.

## WASHED ASHORE

It is easy to appreciate why some mermaids feel out of place, insecure and uneasy on the terrain of land. Without a helping hand they can become lost or lodged on the shores. Their energy field is delicate, but worth protecting. It is not easy for them to call for help when they feel they have been dismissed or judged in the past. Some are reluctant to ask for assistance as they believe it is their calling to hear the cries of others and instead hide away with their tales of woe. Indeed, it is not easy for mermaids to move forward alone on this rigid ground where once they swam in seas of love with their sisters.

Mermaids in their shadow benefit from being aware that they are not operating optimally. Here are some sentiments that if they resonate, suggest you may also be in your shadow:

- Low self-esteem

- Self-deprecating

- Out of place

- Judged

- Misunderstood

- Disempowered

- Lack of confidence

- Anxious

- Trapped

You can start to shift these feelings by entertaining the idea that it is possible to do so. The shift begins with an appreciation that if you want change in your outer life you benefit from learning strategies and techniques to support change in the inner one. The inner world is reflected in outer experiences and not the other way round.

Mermaids have an inner force, a magnetism that guides them to where they are needed. This same energy is reciprocated for them on land because their shine, however well hidden, is sensed by others and guidance and support is forthcoming if they are willing to accept it. When the mermaid is brave enough to engage with the kindness of humans they find that such support inspires and rejuvenates them enough to feel a sense of fluidity again. They do not need to feel that they are stranded on a shore, but instead in an exciting location with the possibilities of new adventures. This is an easier proposition to entertain when you know the location of the hidden treasure that others seek.

The mermaid's journey, or swim, to the light is as individual as a fingerprint. Her journey is her reason for being and her being makes the journey possible. The exact route and the experiences she claims and creates on her way will be in partnership with the rhythm of nature. It is her unique existence that adds to the collective light, making it mesmerising and bright.

## MAGNIFYING REALITY

During a diving trip in the Philippines we were given a magnifying glass. We were urged to slow down and take our time to look at the underwater world in front of us. We were encouraged to notice the subtleties of shape and colour, what moved, and what appeared static, but seldom was. We are so busy in our day to day life that we often miss the present moment with all its nuances - a facial expression, a hunch and other signs that may have encouraged a different reaction if we had but noticed.

In our fast-moving society, people are often so focussed on external manifestations of success such as what we do, what we have, what we look like and what we have achieved, that our emotional plane is often overlooked. An open-hearted self-enquiry into our inner programme can produce new insights into our current responses, fragile alliances, feelings of inadequacy, and reasons for our addictions and our drive to overachieve. It can help us to reevaluate our beliefs, silence the inner critic and find another way. Focussing on the inner world is like exercising a muscle; it requires regular, sometimes painful practice, but it is well worth the effort.

Taking time to reflect on your life is important, both the internal world of your beliefs and what is reflected back in your external world. It is also useful to be clear about what you define as a successful life. This may involve reevaluating and redefining your definition to ensure it is what you want, not what you feel you should want. With such insights it becomes easier to support and develop an inner programme that is in alignment with who you are.

Advice and gentle encouragement is useful, if it resonates, because it is a sign you are ready for a deeper healing and a willingness to engage in your calling. If you don't feel ready the advice will appear irrelevant and is usually ignored or dismissed. Although many people appreciate following a strong lead, mermaids need to find their own channel. They cannot be herded along a path suited for another, however well-intentioned. Mermaids do not need to be saved by something external, they know it's an inside job. When they claim their power as mermaids they know they will not drown.

There are many strategies that can support change so that the mermaid can have the experiences she desires. Emotions are the compass. If used well they help guide you to make the decisions that result in feeling better and hence take you up the vibrational ladder. When in tune with your emotions they indicate when life is in or out of alignment with who you are and where you want to be. However, this intuitive guidance system gets blocked or shuts down due to a series of life events and it takes time and focus to ensure that it is opened up once more. If not, instead of feeling empowered and alive you feel powerless and at the mercy of random events. This can lead to a loss of direction, a lack of energy, fractious relationships and ill health, leaving little appetite to take action when the waves become rough. You cannot totally avoid the effects of the waves and the currents, as they are part of life. But how resilient you are and how quickly you bob back to a floating position and then to riding the crest of your wave is influenced by your inner programme, your sense of self.

We all benefit from considering the messages within and around us. These can coax us to flow with the inevitable changing tides more willingly rather than clinging on as hard as we can in the hope of stability. Like writings in the sand, life changes and the water moved by the tide across the shore demonstrates the opportunities we have to start anew.

When we understand how to access the messages around and within us, we have a guiding system to support our flow. Great insights can be made that will help our choices and move us forward in life once we appreciate our role in shaping our experience and when we are aware of how our world communicates with us. For example, a message delivered through a song you hear on a consistent basis reminds you of a person you have been intending to phone. This message is the nudge you need to turn the thought of phoning into the action of doing. You phone your friend and the serendipity of the exchange leads you to an event you wanted to attend, but couldn't get tickets for. This event becomes significant in moving your present business project forward.

The reflection of life is a tool to support the manifestation of your dreams by ensuring you have the clarity of your own vision, rather than simply accepting what you think is achievable from your past experience.

## PERFECTION IN REFLECTION

The sun was starting to rise. As it was too bright to be looked at directly, I took in the range of beautiful pinks and golds playing off the water and noticed the perfection of the reflection. Just as the sea reflected back the sun with its promise of a new day, with nothing hidden, nothing pushed aside and without judgement, so our experiences reflect back our internal programming.

In their flow mermaids are familiar with a multidimensional approach to existence and swim in harmony with the rhythms of the Universe. In their human form they have slowed down in the fluidity of both body and mind. In their shadow they discover they have become increasingly rigid in their beliefs, often as a protection mechanism. Our beliefs have an impact on how we approach life and what we are prepared to accept. Once we understand how reflection works we can shift our lives gently by altering our belief systems. We can support this by uncovering and understanding the stories that hold us back.

Just as the water's surface reflects back what is above, so there are reflections available that offer insights into what is going on inside of you. These reflections provide a powerful tool for introspection, resulting in an awareness of your beliefs and con-sequential behaviour patterns that need to change in order to achieve a different result. Once appreciated, they offer continuous opportunities to widen your perception and shift your reality. For example, you see people getting promotions everywhere, from your friends and even on your favourite TV programmes, and it makes you feel emotional. You realise this is something you want too, but either hadn't received such opportunities or hadn't recognised them when they did come along. You decide to explore your beliefs about your self-worth, deservingness and your channels to receiving that you are blocking. You find after an inner exploration that you have a belief that you can't have a career and a successful home life. Con-sequently, you had deliberately, albeit unconsciously, chosen not to put yourself forward for a promotion. Once you realise this you start to notice people around you who have satisfying careers and home lives, and choose to believe that you can as well. The resistance to promotion dissolves and you are more willing to put yourself forward, contributing to the likelihood of a new experience.

Once in the habit of being more aware, you can notice the subtleties and the nuances of life. You notice messages within everyday occurrence supporting you to stay on track by being more aligned with your own authenticity. When you are tuned into these messages you also become in tune with the energy of life, flowing with it rather than against it. Just as the surface of the sea is a portal into another world that many individuals never consider, so there are portals into different dimensions all around us, offering messages and insights.

Mermaids, with their empathic nature, have an innate receptivity to realise the gifts contained within life's reflections. Once you dive in and open your communication channels to them you see insights everywhere. For example:

- The repetitive theme of your dramas.

- The dynamics of your relationships.

- The use of your language.

- The conversations you have with yourself and others.

- Events that push your buttons.

- What you see in the mirror.

- The coincidences and serendipities of your life.

- How you feel about life and possibilities.

- How you nurture yourself.

- The repetitive number sequences you see.

- The colours you are drawn to or repelled by.

- Your body language.

- Your diseases.

- Your level of abundance.

## SUSTAINABLE SEAS

Louise Hay was direct and literal with this concept of reflection. She advocated a physical mirror as a tool to learn about your inner landscape by connecting with your inner child (or for us, our inner mermaid).

By communicating with your inner mermaid you gain greater appreciation of your inner voice and programmes that influence how you operate in life. You become more conscious of what judgements you received in the past that you considered to be true and what you were taught. This helps you to appreciate your usual patterns of behaviour and their consequences. You are then better positioned to consciously change your usual response patterns by changing the stories you tell yourself.

Without introspection you find it challenging to make the changes you seek. This is because you have two people influencing your life: you and your inner mermaid. They are out of alignment with each other, with one trying to go with the flow of life and the other dragging you in a different direction out of fear. For instance, if you hope to have a successful advertising business, but believe from past experience that you will fail, you have a counter-belief to your new intention. If you do achieve your goal it often gives no lasting satisfaction or you sabotage the positive outcome before it becomes truly integrated into your life. A reason for this is that your unconscious programming is operating from a belief system that is not yours. It is based on emotional responses learnt in childhood and given by others, which results in your beliefs and decision-making process being in conflict with who you really are and what you truly hope to experience. The dynamic interplay between you and your inner mermaid can be like any other relationship. It may take time and trust or it may be instantaneous; either way, it is a relationship worth engaging in.

Many people seem to come to terms with their inner child quite easily. They appreciate the importance of doing so and are eager to reclaim their control. The mermaid, however, may need to dive deeper. The pain stored within feels too intense and the level of forgiveness needed can seem unthinkable. This is because the sorrow of many lifetimes is, along with ancestral themes, held tightly within their present incarnation. The channels for release are blocked by a strong incoming current of resistance, which can result in the mermaid operating in a dark and lonely place. Some mermaids need more gentle coaxing before they appreciate that their own self-sabotage and victim mentality have contributed to this experience. Once they understand this and trust in the process, they can change as swiftly as the ocean tides.

Through the insights offered by the mermaid it becomes clear that we all have, to different degrees, lost parts of ourselves and our sense of who we are, whether through childhood programming or cultural and social norms. Many people discover that their beliefs and behaviour patterns are not their own preferences, but were given to or demanded from them when they were younger. We can replace these with our own beliefs and regain our alignment and our authenticity.

There are also important messages in the reflections we are reluctant or are unwilling to engage with. These are the beliefs we hold tight, the ideas we will not entertain, the possessions and relationships we will not release. As with other areas in life, if we block the energy flow there are consequences; however, it is possible to gently release resistance before the pressure mounts and becomes more difficult to manage.

Mermaids in their flow are aware of the many reflections offering gifts and take responsibility for using them wisely.

*"Sometimes you dive so deep and you still can't find me," says the inner mermaid. "I will," replies the mermaid, "I will!"*

## SEA-ING YOUR LIFE DIFFERENTLY

Mermaids in their shadow side can be confused or in denial about their empathic gifts. Give yourself time to learn more about how your world communicates with you. This makes it easier to discern the different messages you receive in your day to day living. People have different strengths regarding their mode of communication. Consider learning more about the clair-senses. Dive deep into each so you can feel how they may relate to you. These include:

- Clairvoyance - clear seeing

- Claircognizance - clear knowing

- Clairaudience - clear hearing

- Clairempathy - clear emotional feeling

- Clairgustance - clear tasting

- Clairsentience - clear physical feeling

- Clairtangency - clear touching

- Clairsalience - clear smelling

## CREST OF A WAVE

This chapter explored the importance of your inner mermaid and how your unconscious adherence to past codes impacts your present beliefs and corresponding behavioural patterns.

Chapter four encourages you to examine your behaviour and to cast out what no longer serves you.

## MERMAID MINDSET

*I am your reflection, as you are mine.*

Life can take you in a direction that you don't really want to go. There are reflections everywhere if you are willing to look. Time for reflection may seem time-consuming in a busy world, but it can save time and heartache later. We service our cars, have medical checks and clean our homes, but we don't always appreciate the importance of doing the same with our minds and the programming that influences where we go and how fast we travel.

## MERMAID MOTTOS

Before you journal, write some mermaid mottos to support your motivation. For example:

*I am willing to reflect on situations that I find emotional because by understanding them I move myself forward.*

*I know my outer world is a reflection of my inner programming and I use this to support positive change.*

## EXERCISE

MIRROR WORK

As mentioned earlier, Louise Hay advocated "mirror work" as an effective way of making shifts in your life and as an effective strategy to help you engage directly with your inner child (our inner mermaid) in order to discover how you operate and why. It may feel uncomfortable at first, but if you are not able to see yourself clearly, how will anyone else?

For this exercise, hold a mirror and look into your eyes. Look past your physical attributes and into your soul. Notice any emotions or thoughts that arise. Whilst continuing to look deeply into your eyes, start talking to your inner mermaid with compassion. Make your conversation free of judgment. Ask how she is feeling, and if she has anything to share. Chat with her in positive and encouraging ways. You can make the experience less intense by having fun with your reflection. Give yourself a wink, pull a funny face or give yourself a thumbs up. If this feels strange or challenging, consider how acceptable you have found it to look in the mirror and judge yourself without question. Why not the other way round?

- Research more about mirror work so you can understand how it provides a portal to your belief system and self-esteem.

- Create a daily mirror work routine.

- Consider whether the responses and beliefs of your inner mermaid offer a counter intention, preventing the realisation of your conscious goals.


## SEA-C

CHOICE

When we are offered something new we can block it or dismiss it out of rigidity. Reflect on how you respond to different opportunities. Appreciate also that you may not choose what happens to you in life, but you have a choice over how you respond. With time, practice, and deliberate focus, you can train your responses to situations. Your pattern can change.

Consider turning situations you would have previously seen as negative into more positive ones and be grateful for them by choice.

This will involve you focussing on what you want more of rather than on what you want to experience less. For example, if your friend cancels your lunch appointment, instead of feeling disgruntled, you can be grateful that you now have time to focus on a project you had started.

Consider whether the conversations in your head drive or hinder you. If they are not as you had hoped you have a choice to continue as you do or to change. Approach change one wave at a time, by one choice after another.

- Notice when you block new ideas without consideration.

- Appreciate when you respond negatively to a suggestion without due thought.

- Be aware of when you accept the judgement of others before reflecting on how you feel about it yourself.

- Be open to change and know that it is a choice.

# CHAPTER 3: REFLECTIONS

*A space to journal my thoughts from this chapter…*

_____

_____

_____

_____

_____

_____

_____

_____

_____

_____

_____

_____

_____

_____

_____

_____

_____

_____

_____

_____

_____

_____

_____

_____

# A CONSIDERATION

What tales do you tell yourself that dull your shine?

- Your character
- Your appearance
- Your intellect
- Your lovability
- Your future
- Your past
- Your present

_____

_____

_____

What do you need to do to put the sparkle back in your life?

- Physical changes
- Environmental changes
- Emotional changes
- Other changes

_____

_____

_____

# COMMITMENT AND MY PLAN OF ACTION

What clair-sense will I commit to exploring and using in more depth today?

_____

_____

_____

What is my plan of action for reflection? Write a list of when you will focus inwards, for example, on your inner calm, your inner mermaid or on the events of the day. State also when you will tune into the messages around you, such as hearing repetitive songs or seeing repetitive numbers.

_____

_____

_____

_____

_____

_____

_____

_____

_____

_____

*I commit. Signed:* _____

# Chapter Four

## CASTAWAYS

*"The heart of man is very much like the sea, it has*

*its storms, it has its tides and in its depths*

*it has its pearls too."*

**— Vincent van Gogh, The Letters of**

**Vincent van Gogh**

## MERMAIDS AT SEA

**M**ermaids know they don't thrive when they are anchored down. They are more etheric, designed to flow in the expansiveness of where they dwell. Mermaids understand the turning of the tides, the power of the moon and the strength of the currents. They appreciate there is a time to do and a time to be. Mermaids intuit when to create, when to enjoy and when to let go.

On land, however, many mermaids feel overburdened, as if they are carrying a heavy load. They feel stuck in the trough, too encumbered to ride the waves. If there for any length of time they become tired, scared and respond defensively rather than creatively to life. The tool of reflection offers insights into what could be released to lighten the load and enable a better flow.

## TRAVELLING LIGHT

In their flow mermaids swim effortlessly and without the need for possessions to keep them in one place for any length of time. They have resources within them and the faith that what they require externally will arrive. Mermaids don't procrastinate, nor do they feel they need to achieve everything themselves. They swim from place to place, sharing and receiving the miracles of the sea. They are in alignment with their nature. Such mermaids have dived deep and are savvy at reading the reflections of life, knowing when to clear through and when to clear out.

## A SINKING FEELING

As I was drifting along a sandy channel towards the end of a dive, I noticed the seabed looked surprisingly level. It reminded me of a field of fresh snow, untouched and undisturbed. The sea has amazing mechanisms to clean itself. I have been lucky to encounter many abundant and beautiful reefs. The waves, tides, currents and microbes all work together to move debris and prevent water stagnating, ensuring sustainability. Sadly, there are areas which are not as nature intended. Human activity such as over-fishing, polluting and reclaiming of land has caused changes to the environment. When you see the result of such activities your heart sinks. Environmentalists are raising our awareness of such dangers and are attempting to redress the issues. Special areas have been set up to protect marine life from the detrimental effects and to allow nature time to restore balance rather than head towards impending calamity. Sometimes we need the same level of support and intervention to prevent that sinking feeling within our own lives.

If you feel you are stuck or are struggling to keep afloat, you could benefit from shifting your energy. A spring cleaning of your physical, emotional and spiritual space, a detoxification and reappraisal of your self can help realign you, recharge your batteries and bring back your zest for life. You can do this on a regular basis or when your life appears to have hit rock bottom.

## MERMAID'S IMMERSION

It is important to appreciate that you don't have to be anything other than who you are. It is at the vibration of acceptance and responsibility that the possibility of action becomes more likely. Once action occurs, shifts happen. You can do this in your own way. You can gently immerse yourself into the currents and drift along, using internal as well as external messages to support and guide you.

Give yourself permission to accept what you want and simultaneously release what prevents you from achieving it. Consider releasing what holds you back:

• Physical clutter

• Shame

• Blame

- Fear

- Tears

- Limiting beliefs

- Negative language

- Stress

- Resentment

- Negative judgment

- Over-committing

- Perfectionism

## ALL HANDS ON DECK

On one dive, I noticed everything seemed larger. I saw huge clams and witnessed the swiftness with which they closed at the first sign of danger. I could imagine people getting trapped in them due to their size. I tried to stay and see how long it took them to open again, but the gentle current moved me to the next astounding sight and the clams became dots in the distance. I thought about how easy it is to clam up and how many mermaids have done so. Some real sense of danger presented itself and they shut down. Some never truly opened up again, remaining in their shells with their sadness and fears. Today a gentle message from the Universe whispers that it is time to give life another go and open up once more.

If the deck is clear, the ship can move forward with purpose and ease, untethered and free of hurdles, allowing space for each person to move and operate as appropriate. The deck floor itself benefits from being unimpeded, but the barnacles under the ship, once cleared, can also prevent an unnecessary drag. The link between your physical possessions and your emotional state and vice-versa has long been documented. It was through the work of Denise Linn, a world-acclaimed expert in feng shui and space clearing, that I first became aware of the importance of making space in my life so there was room for something new to arrive. Many people appreciate the need to clean up, reorganise and throw out what they no longer need. Holding onto things that no longer serve you clogs the natural flow and results in a drag, stagnation and eventually a blockage. For the mermaid it's beneficial to look into your emotional paraphernalia as well as your physical possessions.

A deliberate focus on simultaneously casting out and opening yourself up to the world again can be scary, but it is a transformational experience well worth the effort. Knowing how can be overwhelming, but luckily there are many choices. Having many hands on deck so you can approach this in several ways at once is useful.

*"Some people want to attain new heights. I want to dive deep!' giggled the mermaid.*

## TEARS AND FEARS

The batfish played with our bubbles as we started to ascend into shallow waters. I watched as they confidently came closer and closer to my buddy's head. They seemed comfortable with us. This was in marked contrast to the hawkfish I had seen earlier, clinging to the reef, or the blennies ready to dive for cover at the slightest sense of danger. It's understandable that some mermaids on land feel scared in an environment that seems unfamiliar to them.

It is not easy to reveal your gifts and sing your song in the world if you are fearful and tearful. A lack of self-esteem makes the mermaid reluctant to use their voice and fear can prevent the realisation of their dreams. Hiding away no longer seems a viable option. The call for action continues even louder, becoming too strong to ignore, and is accompanied by an intense sense of sadness over unfulfilled dreams. It is time to dry the tears and tame the fears. It may not be possible to disregard them all, but you can rock their boat of complacency within your life.

Mermaids have cried many tears for themselves and for those who have lived before and will live after them. At times it seems that they want to flood the world in the hope that the water will soothe the pain. Tears feel like the only way they can release intense emotions. Through self-exploration you can bring the stories to the surface. You can transmute them into messages of hope and discover another way to operate. This doesn't mean you condone what happened, but that you release the energy that binds you to the past.

It is the same with your fears. If you can rock them about a bit, you see them for what they are. Some are strategies that protected you in the past, but no longer serve you in the present. Some fears are merely apprehension for an unknown future that can be reframed, whilst others are someone else's beliefs that are not applicable to you and can be released.

It is easy to appreciate why mermaids self-sabotage if they are fearful. Some mermaids criticise themselves first, in the fear that they will get criticised or ridiculed by others. Other mermaids dart away from situations or commitments, fearful that they might get shunned or abandoned if they stay. Life does not need to be so painful, contained or controlled. It is easier to go with the flow or to release at times, to embrace the uncertainty with faith and curiosity, rather than with tears and fears.

## CHOPPY WATERS OF BLAME AND SHAME

Engaging in a deep conversation about who you are and why you respond as you do is useful. It results in identifying what needs to go. In addition to the tears and fears, many mermaids have issues around blame and shame.

Due to past experiences some mermaids have boundaries that are either so strong they are restrictive or not strong enough, leaving them vulnerable to the demands of others. Mermaids would do well to reappraise their boundaries, often a response to blame and shame, to ensure that they are appropriate for their specific and valid requirements, caring for their energy for optimal health. Anything less will make them ill.

Gay Hendricks, a contributor to the fields of relationship transformation and body-mind therapies, coins in his book, *The Big Leap: Conquer Your Hidden Fear and Take Life to the Next Level*, an "upper limit" on what we are prepared to achieve and receive. He argues that we create our own limitations about what is possible through our belief systems. We then become disappointed when we can't achieve our goals which are beyond them. To prevent feeling this way, many people stop trying and instead tolerate the status quo as a protective mechanism against a sense of failure they feel when trying and not achieving.

Holding on to hurtful memories and beliefs that don't serve you curtails your energy and triggers you to repeat self-sabotaging behaviour. It is useful to explore your emotional response to situations and uncover the original story. For many gentle souls this clearing has several layers including the personal, the social and the ancestral.

Part of the path of self-acceptance and feeling you have a right to have your needs met is through understanding your temperament using a supportive definition. As founders of "The Quiet Revolution" advocate, the next generation of quiet children will benefit by being raised to know their strengths. For those already grown, it can be a longer readjustment to appreciate that your disposition is both healthy and socially acceptable. Understanding that healthy boundaries are essential, that solitude is a catalyst for innovation and that the world benefits from deep thinkers are healthy beliefs to have. They can help cast out blame or shame accepted in the past for seeming inappropriate or antisocial. Appreciating your needs and feeling you have a right to have them met results in you being more resilient to the judgment of others who operate in a different way. Honour your need for personal space and a level of privacy because you understand that you operate best when you do so.

A difficult issue for mermaids is finding a way of satisfying their need for space with the demand for their company from others. As mermaids are happy being alone they can be perceived by some people as being antisocial or even unfriendly. Mermaids do not feel comfortable with large groups, preferring quality conversations in smaller and more intimate settings. That said, they often feel guilty about establishing strong boundaries as they had not previously appreciated the importance of recharging their own batteries or feeling they had the right to do so. In the end this compromises their health. Mermaids do well when they have healthy boundaries in place. For example:

- Make your diary a new best friend and visit it regularly, ensuring you have adequate spaces between arrangements.

- Limit physical interactions when arranging events by texting instead.

- Consider whether your commitments are vital or if you are just people pleasing.

- Organise get-togethers in small groups rather than larger crowds.

- Establish your right to protect your energy level as a priority.

## JETTISONING JUDGEMENTS

Once you have placed the magnifying glass on your tears and fears and your blames and shames, the next step is to figure out how you can release the judgements, often first felt in childhood, that bring no benefit by remaining in adulthood.

Judgements can be harsh and detrimental to your well-being. It is interesting to notice how often we make judgements and then make decisions from them. As Dr. Libby Weaver, an internationally acclaimed nutritional biochemist, author and speaker, explains in her book, *Exhausted to Energized: Dr. Libby's Guide to Living Your Life with More Energy*, we are "meaning-makers." It is the meanings we put to events that become our stories and often our ill-serving beliefs. These stories need to be released if we are to create new realities. Failure is an event, not an identity. If something doesn't work out, it doesn't work out. It doesn't mean you are a failure as a person. You can pick yourself up, learn from the experience and take another step forward with renewed knowledge and optimism. It is important not to let past failure break your spirit for future success. Instead, become more comfortable with failure as a tool for improvement rather than the cause of stagnation due to harsh judgements and your fear. When something doesn't work as planned, reflect with curiosity rather than judgement as to how you behaved and why. Then learn from it.

In life we have experiences. We can enjoy them, exaggerate them or feel let down by them. Notice:

- When you add a story onto an action. For instance, the action of missing the bus becomes accompanied by a story that forms a disempowering judgement. For example, "I missed the bus *because* I am stupid." Instead state, "I missed the bus. I will leave home earlier next time!"

- When you add a generalisation to a situation. For example, "I missed the bus because I am *always* unlucky!" Instead state, "I missed the bus. This can happen!"

Who do you blame? Why do you feel blame? What is your original story? You may not be responsible for delivering the reason for such feelings, but as indicated previously, it's a choice to remain stuck with them, whether that choice is conscious or unconscious. Once you appreciate that as an adult you are responsible for yourself, you can start to look at things differently in order to release the pain and the blocks, thereby allowing your life to flow better for you.

## STRESS

The consequence of too much stress in our lives is widely known. In her book, *Rushing Woman's Syndrome: The Impact of a Never-Ending To-Do List and How to Stay Healthy in Today's Busy World,* Dr. Libby Weaver offers insights into why many people are experiencing such high levels of stress, perceived or real, and why the stress button remains on even if the actual stress has been removed. Her work was a breakthrough in my understanding. Rushing here and there doesn't always deserve the pat on the back, with people thanking you for all you've done. On the contrary, she argues, being overly busy and the consequential stress this brings could be considered an ailment of our time.

Feeling stressed makes you tired; it also disturbs your sleep so that you don't wake up refreshed. Over time, chronic stress and anxiety contributes to adrenal burnout and autoimmune diseases, as well as over-eating. Even when you are watching your diet, stress causes chemical changes in your body that causes it to hold on to fat.

A common source of stress is the feeling that you are responsible for doing everything for everyone. This is exhausting and clogs up the channels for joy. If you are constantly rushing around in an attempt to please others or feel overly responsible for them, it is important to look at the underlying need for this. It is also useful to have strategies to relieve the sensation of stress instantly. This can be as simple as a few slow deep and deliberate breaths that calm the nervous system enough for you to gain conscious awareness of what you are doing. On a longer term basis, try to shift your default mode from rushing around to deliberate engagement with the present moment, with built-in time for reflection. Mermaids respond well to affirming "I have all the time in the world!" Release yourself from the pressure that you need to be everywhere or that everything needs to be done immediately, perfectly and by you. Look at what is important, prioritise and delegate. When you are facing deadlines to get things done, be sure to take time to recharge later on, before your health forces you to slow down.

## GUT REACTION

As some mermaids are prone to feeling stressed, they are also likely to have sensitive guts and consequently will experience challenges in their digestive systems. It is easy to understand why, considering that the gut is the intuitive centre of our being. Without supportive boundaries and self-care rituals in place to calm the nervous system and preserve energy levels, these issues will be exacerbated.

A healthy relationship with food is critical. Becoming land-bound can cause some teething issues, which arise in the form of inflammation in the body. If you suffer from gut issues, you want to discover which foods nourish you and which foods take a toll on your general wellbeing and energy levels. It may take a lot of trial and error for mermaids to determine what suits their biochemistry, but it is well worth the effort.

I turn again to the work of Dr. Libby Weaver, specifically the online course based on her book, *Accidentally Overweight: The 9 Elements That Will Help You Solve Your Weight-Loss Puzzle.* She stresses the importance of healing the liver and the adrenals. With more energy, there is more determination and enthusiasm to continue to feel good. The knowledge she shared was not new to me, but the gentle and supportive way she delivered it empowered me to action the advice and engage in a more mindful eating practice. She didn't enforce a system, but gently guided, reminded and explained why the body needs a time of readjustment in order to return to a place where it can efficiently and effectively deal with what we eat. Her method encourages us to appreciate that the body isn't always responsible for what has happened to it, rather it is the manifestation of our choices.

## NEGATING NEGATIVE LANGUAGE

Developmental biologist Dr. Bruce Lipton was also a lifeline to me in those early days of inner diving. In his groundbreaking book, *The Biology of Belief: Unleashing the Power of Consciousness, Matter & Miracles*, he explained that we are not victims of heredity, but the masters of our biology. He argues it is our perception of the environment that controls our lives and health. It is what we believe, think and how we speak that are vital in the expression of our genes. This was my first introduction to epigenetics, and it opened my eyes to the role I play in my life experiences.

I realised that it is not enough to detox yourself from the negative stories running through your mind; you must also be aware of the language that exits your mouth and enters your ears. Language both reflects and triggers your inner world, which is why it is important to be vigilant with your words. Consider the conversations you have and the type of language you use, including the expressions you use on a regular basis, whether family idioms, cultural beliefs or song lyrics. Are these uplifting and empowering or negative and self-defeating? The goal is to catch yourself when using neg-affirmations and instead turn them into positive mermaid mottos. For example:

- *Money doesn't grow on trees!* becomes *I receive abundance from everywhere!*

- *You can't teach an old dog new tricks!* becomes *I am always learning new things!*

## SEA-ING YOUR LIFE DIFFERENTLY

Release yourself from operating from a place of overtired, over-committed, over-worked and with an expectation of perfection. Find compassion for yourself and honour your power of choice; your freedom to choose and to choose again.

When you understand that life can change, you can take stock and consider your role in making this happen. You can look at what needs to go and then decide how you'll do it. Once you own your power you blame less and take responsibility more.

- What are the main things in your life that you'd like to liberate?

- Start to notice your inner conversations. Are they uplifting or demotivating? Who is responsible for your thoughts? Are you happy with them?

- Become more aware of what is happening in and around you. Notice when you blame other people and when you blame yourself. Also take notice of when things do not carry a charge.

- Reflect back on situations where you felt you gave your power away. Although it may have seemed the best action to take at the time, can you now see that there could have been a different outcome if your response or approach was different?

## THE CREST OF A WAVE

This chapter looked at the need to cast away areas of your life that no longer serve you. As with the sea, the rhythm of life means that change is inevitable, but sometimes it is useful to make the change before a sudden storm shakes everything up and makes an enforced disposal necessary.

Chapter five looks at ensuring healthy practises are in place.

## MERMAID MINDSET

*I show you where I am broken so you can become whole.*

It took a while before I accepted that I was carrying an unnecessary load that weighed me down. As I released unhealthy habits and limiting beliefs I felt lighter, more flexible and more energised than I had in years. It was only by feeling this restored health did I realise how restricted I had become. I noticed that as I let go of my energetic burden, my body weight reduced as well.

## MERMAID MOTTO

Before you take time to journal, reflect on some mermaid mottos. You are welcome to dive into mine.

*I am willing to detox my life for my higher good.*

*I release what no longer serves me to create space for what does.*

*It is easy for me to make choices and take the actions necessary for my wellbeing.*

*My inner self talks to me and I listen.*

## EXERCISE

DECLUTTER

Decluttering alters the vibration of your being. Your exercise for this chapter is to start the process of decluttering. It can feel over-whelming if you're not sure where to start. One way is to write out a list and to break it down into smaller, more manageable tasks, such as:

- A kitchen cupboard
- Your emails
- Your wardrobe

As you declutter affirm:

*I declutter my life and my life feels good.*

*As I declutter I feel the positive shifts this makes.*

*I trust that as I release, I attract new and supportive things towards me.*

## SEA-C

CONGRATULATE

Sustained, healthy choices are easier to make when you are feeling good about yourself. If you have made a bad decision, berating yourself for a lack of judgement isn't likely to produce the positive vibe necessary for you to make a better quality decision next time. It is time to start forgoing the harsh judgments and instead use self-congratulations as a tool for change.

As you go about your day find reasons to be cheerful. Acknowledge what you have done. Celebrate the wins, both large and small.

*When I congratulate myself I support a high vibration.*

*When I acknowledge what I am pleased with I attract more of it.*

*When I congratulate myself, I feel motivated to do more.*

# CHAPTER 4: CASTAWAYS

*A space to journal my thoughts from this chapter…*

# A CONSIDERATION

What are you doing that may be impeding your progress?

- Over-achieving
- Over-protecting
- Over-giving
- Over-working
- Over-denying
- Over-worrying

Do you hold on to things out of fear?

What do you hold on to that is making you sink rather than float?

What would you like to get rid of, but feel you can't, and why?

What needs to go that you could do something about?

_____

_____

_____

_____

_____

_____

_____

_____

_____

_____

_____

_____

# COMMITMENT AND MY PLAN OF ACTION

What will I commit to letting go of today?

_____
_____
_____

What is my plan of action for decluttering my life?

_____
_____
_____
_____
_____
_____
_____
_____
_____
_____
_____
_____
_____
_____
_____
_____

*I commit. Signed:* _____

# Chapter Five

## THE MERMAID'S TAIL

*"Darwin may have been quite correct in his*

*theory that man descended from the apes of the*

*forest, but surely woman rose from the frothy sea,*

*as resplendent as Aphrodite on*

*her scalloped chariot."*

**— Margot Datz, A Survival Guide for**

**Landlocked Mermaids**

## MERMAIDS' TALES OF TAILS

The benefits of self-care are well documented. If you are drowning you need to save yourself before you can help anyone else. Self-care is not indulgent, it's essential. If you don't feel good about your life or are living with burnout and a sense of negative inevitability, I hope the earlier chapters have indicated the importance of uncovering and releasing the tales you tell yourself so you can shift your life experiences. This chapter encourages you to fill the space you've created with activities and routines that produce a high vibrational feeling.

## MORPHING MERMAIDS

We often read about the importance of good food and exercise in a self-care regime, but less about ensuring our true embodiment and empowerment. This involves a deeper dive.

I was floating above a coral bed, my eyes on the sharks in front. They were gliding back and forth, guarding their territory, maintaining their boundaries and demonstrating to all that encountered them that they are the top of the food chain. The sharks seemed to command their space within the water as they moved through it, as if the medium for their manoeuvre was immaterial. I imagined above them, below them and swimming alongside them were mermaids, belonging to this sea community every bit as much as the sharks, just operating in a different way. Mermaids in their flow embrace the water knowing that this liquid supports them as they move up, down and around with grace and enjoyment.

When you appreciate how you operate, both within yourself and within the environment you find yourself, you have more scope to shift your experiences as you require.

Mermaids in their shadow often need to work on self-acceptance in a way that their goddess sisters may not appreciate. Unlike these sisters, birthing into this dimension isn't always a complete process. The result is that some mermaids feel disconnected within themselves, dissociated with the world and full of bodily ailments. As a result they are prone to letting their energy wane and, instead of an energised flow, life can seem a constant struggle. Becoming fully present and consequently more empowered involves becoming fully embodied. The result of this metamorphism is more enjoyment for the magnificence of the Earth walk experience.

## EMBODIMENT

During my self-help and personal development work I learnt a lot about the importance of grounding. Indeed, it was suggested that I walked around with a tanzanite stone and wear brown clothes. There is an understanding that the best way to experience a good life is to be truly present in it, literally, to stand firm on Mother Earth first, then access your connection to the higher dimensions. In my previous book, *Spiritual Seas: Diving into Life,* I explained the cosmic joke that being an air sign and a dreamer I aligned myself with the sky and the stars. However, all the focus on grounding encouraged by my fellow Earthlings took me soaring down so fast that I didn't stop on Earth's rich soil, but plunged to the seabed. All things and all places, including the sky and the sea, are mirrors and reflections that can be used to support our understanding of our life experience. I had questioned how the disposition of the mermaid is different from her land sisters and, as such, I had been given a completely different experience to fully understand such differences. Maybe it wasn't a cosmic joke after all; maybe I had just returned home.

For mermaids living on land it's important to feel in their body and to accept and integrate their different parts. Being grounded on the Earth and fully embodied are steps that are often missing when discussing self-acceptance and encouraging empowerment. It was not until I discovered Melissa Sandon, a truly inspirational woman who is passionate about the power of rebirthing to fully appreciate our soul work, that I understood these requirements. To feel present in your body and on land, and to feel worthy of this opportunity, is especially interesting for those with a mermaid disposition. In their shadow side they can feel a deep-rooted shame or unease at being in a rigid skeletal container and having lost their glittery tail. It takes inner work, negotiation, integration and a whole lot of forgiveness before there can be an appreciation and enjoyment that a body is a temple rather than a cage.

Once mermaids accept that they are in human form they appreciate more fully the importance of respecting and nurturing their bodies by positive and healthy rituals. Unlike our souls, our bodies are privy to the laws of the land and need nourishment, rest and exercise to stay fit and healthy and to ensure they are the best container for the soul to temporarily reside within. Mermaids respond quickly to life on land when they are fully embodied and have rid themselves of any tales they tell themselves about being anything less than who they really are.

*"Although I'm from the sea and you're from the land, we're both sisters," exclaimed the mermaid, "We're derived from the same love!"*

## EMPOWERMENT

The fish danced in front of us in a flash of colour, shape and design. There were fish with long noses and short noses. There were fish with vertical stripes, horizontal stripes, with mosaic or spotted patterns, in fact, every design you could imagine. They were vibrant and they all seemed to belong.

Studying dive books helped me look at the sea life with more purpose and clarity. I started to give myself a goal for each dive, for instance, to notice the shape of the fish tails or the shape of their mouths. It was interesting to see how the different designs enabled the fish to operate in specific ways. The combination of reading about the fish and then experiencing what they looked like took me along a learning journey that was enjoyable and rewarding. I realised I had used this technique for my own self-awareness.

Once you understand and appreciate your own temperament and attributes, it's easier to own your power. Given their years of experiencing multidimensionally and feeling unintentionally or deliberately judged for it, it's easy to see why mermaids may either mistrust their own communication channels or lack the trust in others to share their true nature. Empowerment is about releasing the judgements that make you feel unworthy and accepting the pieces of yourself again. As you do this, visibility and speaking your truth are no longer as challenging.

Many mermaids never fully trust themselves or others because as children they were taught not to share information about the world that was received through means other than their five senses. This caused a mismatch between their reality and the opinions of those in authority. Such a mismatch results in confusion over whether they can trust their own discernment, as well as feeling they have displeased others with their sharing. Over time they lean to hide who they are and keep their observations to themselves.

A mermaid's self-esteem increases once she validates her own view of reality again. This means trusting in her multidimensional communications. Open discussions about such viewpoints on the internet, in books and films can help, as you come to realise other people also experience in this way. There is more appreciation of taking note of your intuition and gut reactions. Reappraise what you have been taught and what you believe.

Part of being truly embodied and empowered is owning your light. It's about discarding the tarnish that dulls your shine. It's knowing what nourishes you emotionally, mentally, physically and spiritually to operate at optimal glow. Once you know who you are and how you operate you appreciate that you have as much right to be on the planet as others. You can disperse all perceived limitations within you and access higher dimensional information which results in a flow of abundance that defies the land's law of cause and effect. By doing so you assist others as well as yourself.

Consider afresh key attributes that you may have felt were dismissed or undervalued when you were a child. For example, being told you were too:

- Intuitive

- Mysterious

- Empathic

- Sensitive

- Perceptive

- Profound

- Different

What are your views now?


## RESUSCITATING MERMAIDS

Mermaids benefit from taking stock of who they are and how they feel. Feeling tired and washed out is not a normal state to be. To feel revitalised it is important to resuscitate the mermaid and to restore her from being stranded horizontal on the beach to being free and flexible to explore the land.

Dr. Libby Weaver suggests that we see vitality as the currency of health. She is concerned about the quality of life that many people have and feels they are spending too little time living and far too much time dying. Being tired, overwhelmed and in discomfort is not how we are meant to be. Everything is more difficult when we are exhausted. It is what we do every day that impacts our health rather than what we do occasionally. She believes in doing things consistently rather than perfectly and like Louise Hay, she advocates the benefit of self-care that follows self-love, for we need to feel we are worthy of such care. Appreciate that if a body part or trait frustrates you, it is a messenger with valuable information to explore. Clear the beliefs that no longer serve you and adopt new beliefs and behaviours that support the change you desire.

Dr. Christine Northrup also has a lot to share about reclaiming our health and vitality. Her recent course, *Dodging Energy Vampires,* emphasises the importance of healing old wounds by considering key issues and then claiming their opposite resolution. For instance, if you feel unsafe due to abandonment issues you would focus on healing the field of commitment inside of you so you are not as triggered by the outside world. If betrayal was more your issue, you would focus on loyalty. If it were shame, she suggests you would benefit from focussing on experiencing light and humour. People crave intimacy, and if you don't receive it from others, Dr. Christine Northrup advocates giving it, as well as recognising it in yourself. She offers five attributes that support adult relationships and five mantras that can help acknowledge these needs in yourself. These are perfect tools to support your mirror work.

| ATTRIBUTE | MANTRA |
| --- | --- |
| Attention | I see you |
| Appreciation | I value you |
| Approval | I accept you |
| Affection | I love you |
| Allowing | I trust you |

Mel Robbins, a renowned motivational and keynote speaker, offers her "five-second rule" to support our self-care. This technique involves taking action within five seconds of thinking about something we plan to do. Mel Robbins explains that when our thoughts and feelings are at odds with what we hope to be doing, our feelings win due to the way our brains are wired. A way I have incorporated this into my life is by having everything ready for my daily walk or swim. This way, when the alarm clock goes off I don't need to think or make a choice. I jump out of bed and am ready instantly, as if there is no alternative action to take. The clothes are on, I'm out the house and the exercise has begun before the brain can start to self-sabotage the intention.

Once you are aware of what you are doing and take responsibility for your part in it, you are more able to anticipate the likely results of continuing as you presently do. As a consequence, if you decide you want a change, you start taking action. You reduce or eliminate negative and unhealthy choices and reinstate or introduce new healthier ones. Research indicates that it takes around a month to start or break a habit. You can change your taste buds, feel stifled if you don't get a daily dose of fresh air and crave your energy high from your regular exercise routine. When it's a habit the action becomes easier to sustain. Be kind to yourself. Setting up self-care routines you enjoy will allow you to recharge your energy so you can use it in productive and enjoyable ways.

## SAFE SEAS

When the channel for change is open, life flows. Block the channel and stagnation occurs. With time, the tension mounts until it unblocks automatically by an enforced release. See the signposts, action the synchronicities and allow the energising flow of change to vitalise you without the need for such disruption.

I heard once about experiments conducted in fish tanks. A partition was placed, restricting the fishes' movement between one side of the tank to the other. After some time the partition was removed, but the fish still kept to "their side" of the tank. Is it your time to move beyond past restrictions and into the possibilities of the future?

Ensuring a level of safety is essential to the mermaid's well-being. This sense of safety is strengthened as the mermaid feels more validated and accepted in this world. In its healthy form a need for safety is there to protect us. In its unhealthy form it stops us truly living and it depletes our energy levels. Some new opportunities are dangerous whilst others are just unfamiliar. If we confront our discomfort and try new things we develop and change as an individual. Mermaids were not designed to hide or be contained. In their element they swim free, living in the moment and sharing the gifts that truly living brings with those around them. In their shadow side they limit their experiences as it feels safer to stay with the familiar. Not engaging fully with the world often begins as a misplaced strategy to ensure safety, and results in stronger walls of containment.

Appreciating your own traits will empower you to push gently on these boundaries and embrace new endeavours. Start by incorporating into your life the kinds of activities and rituals that will help you recharge your batteries and maintain a healthy body and mind. Start to engage with your environment and integrate with your community. Some mermaids find the competitive side of sports and team games an alien concept and collaborative ones energetically draining. However, there are many other activities, solitary and otherwise, that could help them release stress, support their health and integrate with the world they live in. I personally have found swimming to be a game changer. Consider:

- Water sports such as swimming, diving, sailing or rowing

- Walking, hiking, exploring
- Yoga, meditation and other mindful practices
- Cinema, theatre, music
- Book clubs, reading or listening to books
- Online courses

## REFRESHING WATER

As mermaids, we have a special infinity with water; we find it a refreshing way to support health and well-being, whether we are in it, on it or drinking it. Of course, we are not alone in this; in fact, water has been important throughout history for healing, detoxing and renewal, and the seaside has long been considered a place to go for medical and emotional healing. The expansive and hypnotic nature of the sea entices the onlooker to become reacquainted with the vastness of where they live and with the awe and wonder of nature.

In his book, *Blue Mind: The Surprising Science That Shows How Being Near, In, On, or Under Water Can Make You Happier, Healthier, More Connected, and Better at What You Do*, Wallace J Nichols writes about the advantage for humans (and mermaids) that water offers. He demonstrates how our proximity to water can improve performance, increase calm, diminish anxiety and increase professional success. He discusses how blue minds are programmed to belong to something bigger than ourselves. He encourages people to reconnect with themselves, those they love, and the special places they care about, and get into water at every opportunity. If you are pressed for time or are not in close proximity to natural water, choose instead to have a bath or take a shower to wash off the day and to soothe tired and sore muscles. Remember also to stay hydrated by drinking plenty of water as well.

## SUCCESSFUL SEAS

An important realisation for many mermaids is that they don't have to do new things perfectly; there is, however, value in trying new things. It is no secret that being closed to ideas, mistrusting advice and being inflexible to different approaches makes positive change difficult. If you have been procrastinating, however, you have not totally blocked the channel of change. If or when you do take action, even if you make mistakes or make choices that were not as good as you had hoped, you are in a better place to reassess and make a better, more informed decision next time.

As I dived deeper into my understanding of my mermaid's traits, I realised the importance of both opening myself up to new ideas and engaging with them on a practical level to stretch my boundaries. Learning about ideas and strategies is interesting; actioning and integrating these ideas is life-changing. Introverts do well to know how to recharge their energy levels so they can use their energy in exciting ways. Empaths also do well when they learn how to protect their energy field so they are not as susceptible to the emotions of others. It is not about isolation or hoarding your energy, but about gently coaxing yourself to engage with life and all its amazing opportunities.

Think of our energy like the waves in the sea. These waves are part of the universal dance and a response to the forces of above. There are times they build up, times they come crashing down and times they stabilise out, gently merging in harmony with the water around them. Just like the waves support the continued momentum and sustainability of the water, our energy supports us. And just like the waves are part of the water, we are meant to live as part of life, not apart from it. As we discussed earlier, when you find yourself rejecting ideas and opportunities, consider:

- Why am I blocking this and what is it that I am trying to protect myself from?

- What is the worst that could happen if I did accept this chance, and what is the best?

- Do I need to be so inflexible that what I had planned takes precedence over what the Universe has presented to me?

Sometimes it helps to know that if you agree to an opportunity and make arrangements with other people there are ways to protect yourself. For example:

- Be clear and honest with your friends about your timeframes before you are at the event.

- Learn and experiment with self-care ideas that increase your vitality and support the sustainability of your energy levels so you can spend more time enjoying activities with others.

- Plan recharging time before the event and then remind yourself during the event that in a few hours you will have time alone to rejuvenate and restore.

- Give yourself time out and chance to move around by making or taking a real or pretend phone call, going to the restroom, offering to do event-related errands such as collecting an object from the car.

- Befriend others on the introversion scale so you all go home early.

- Simply excuse yourself and head home.


## SEA-ING YOUR LIFE DIFFERENTLY

We often struggle on in the same way, blind to the repercussions of our own negative rituals. Once you see your life differently you can establish healthier rituals, positive boundaries and protect your energy levels and emotional well-being more zealously. Once you feel worthy of being alive you feel more deserving of such care. You also feel more empowered to take the action that will support a happier and more energised you. Consider:

- What healthier routines could you incorporate into your day?

- Where could you reduce the need to please others so you have more time and energy to spend on achieving your own priorities?

- What practice could you engage in that would make you feel less stressed and more calm?

## CREST OF A WAVE

In this chapter we explored the importance of self-care as it applies to the mermaid. The benefit of this creates a ripple effect on various aspects of your life and on those around you. When you are in a good place, you have more energy, vitality and more compassion for the needs of others. You see serendipity that supports your flow so you are living, not merely surviving.

The next chapter explores my personal story as it relates to the chapter titles of this book. I hope to demonstrate that the treasure is you and how important it is to accept this and to allow yourself to shine.

## MERMAID MINDSET

*I am in a temporary physical form, but my spirit is eternal.*

Our body exists in a place where the law of cause and effect applies; it is also where the soul temporarily resides. Our soul is eternal and operates from a space where miracles dwell. When you become embodied and empowered you can play with the laws of both realms.

You also realise how important it is to care for your body, if only because it contains such precious cargo.

When you appreciate this, there is a renewed desire to stay healthy. Through steady action you can support yourself physically, emotionally and spiritually. Through self-care practices you can become lighter in every sense. When your body is in a better place, your soul rejoices.

## MERMAID MOTTOS

Before you take time to journal, reflect on some mermaid mottos.

*I am willing to look after my energy.*

*I am safe.*

*I am worthy of being alive and feeling alive.*

## EXERCISE

CROWD-OUT

When you discover something that you want to change it can be easier and more successful to "crowd-out" the habit rather than giving it up. For instance, if you want to eat in a more healthy way, introduce healthy foods you enjoy rather than focussing on eliminating the ones that are not healthy. Consider:

- What healthy foods can I include into my diet that will improve my energy levels?

- What self-care rituals can I schedule on a regular basis?

- What activities can I engage in that would support the recharging of my energy levels and my connection with the world?

- What positive statements or actions can I use if I find myself about to make an unhealthy choice?

## SEA-C

CONSEQUENCE

Consequences are the outcomes of decisions in our world. In our human experience these are seen as cause and effect. In the soul world miracles are the consequence of deciding something and this works on a totally different dimension. As mermaids we can access both. Appreciate the consequences of your actions, but also appreciate what can become reality by feeling that it already has. When we accept ourselves we feel worthy of receiving. When we are happy with who we are and value our place on this Earth we realise our power for change.

- What would be the consequences for yourself and others if you felt you were worthy of taking care of?

- What would be the consequences for yourself and others if you had more vitality and felt more optimistic?

# CHAPTER 5: THE MERMAID'S TAIL

*A space to journal my thoughts from this chapter…*

_____

_____

_____

_____

_____

_____

_____

_____

_____

_____

_____

_____

_____

_____

_____

_____

_____

_____

_____

_____

_____

_____

_____

_____

_____

_____

_____

_____

# A CONSIDERATION

What stories were you told as a child that disempower you today?

What qualities have you hidden and how can these be uncovered?

What dreams did you have that have been lost along the way?

What scares you about life?

What excites you about life?

What legacy did you hope to leave to the world?

What makes you laugh now and what used to make you laugh?

What games did you play as a child?

What gives you joy now?

If there were no constraints, how would you spend your time?

_____

_____

_____

_____

_____

_____

_____

_____

_____

_____

_____

_____

# COMMITMENT AND MY PLAN OF ACTION

What specific self-care routine will I commit to introducing today?

_____

_____

_____

What is my plan of action for encouraging my own empowerment?

_____

_____

_____

_____

_____

_____

_____

_____

_____

_____

_____

_____

_____

_____

*I commit. Signed:* _____

# Chapter Six

## TREASURE

*"Remember that wherever your heart is, there you will find your treasure."*

— **Paulo Coelho**, **The Alchemist**

## MERMAID'S TREASURE

A sense of adventure begins with the realisation of where the treasure resides. Once you appreciate it is with you, you claim your power. When awareness and action collaborate, change occurs and new creations expand the realm of further possibilities. When the mermaid accepts her power and her place on land she enjoys her own life experience, fulfils her purpose and connects with others, radiating out light in ever extending circles. After all, wasn't that the reason for her birth?

This chapter would logically be placed at the end of the book, but my mermaid was very clear and idiosyncratic; she wanted it here!


## LIFE AT THE SURFACE

During the early part of my life I felt judged and labelled. Through a series of encounters and, more recently by learning about empaths and introverts, I have been able to understand myself better. I have a greater appreciation of how I operate and how best to safeguard my energy and emotions to ensure that my nervous system is not compromised. I am more open with my thoughts and opinions and I am more aware of whether these are mine or borrowed from other people. I engage happily with others, discussing issues with enthusiasm and knowing I have a right to do so. In the end, I realised that however many labels I had been given in the past, the choice to keep them or release them was mine.

Just as I have released many of these labels, I have also set my mermaid free. She still swims with me on occasions, but her mission is complete. She has supported my progress towards embodiment, empowerment and liberation. Her hope was never that I would remain with or as her, but that I would gain awareness to enjoy my life on Earth.

Flat-footed, with a lisp, a range of learning problems and little spacial awareness or dexterity, I felt ill-equipped for life on land. I remember being given a pair of heavy brown shoes, built up inside to address my foot shape. They were cumbersome to wear and I hated the drabness of their colour and shape. They were a far cry from the flexible glamour of a mermaid's tail! Although I wore them for what seemed an age, they did little to rectify the problem; they did, however, do much to dampen my spirit. It was the same with my speech. I had four years with a speech therapist before she walked out on me in frustration, shouting as she left that she could do nothing for me. That wasn't completely true – she had managed to further lower my self-confidence when speaking to others. My dentist did try to help. I had too many teeth for the size of my mouth, and he took quite a few out. This didn't seem to make much difference. It was just another painful experience for a child who seemed a little lost on the shores of life. Ultimately, it would be my mother who assisted me in articulating my words.

## DIVING DEEP

If you feel you are unworthy, why would you believe you are worthy of experiencing a good life? Once you start to dive deep and appreciate the importance of your belief system, life unfolds for you as majestically and as miraculously as the waves in the ocean that rise and fall.

I completed my advanced diving certificate many years ago, which allowed me to dive at a greater depth than my first certification permitted. Slowly, but consistently, my instructor prepared me for the next depth progression. In this way I could get used to the feeling, the slight drag on the regulator as I inhaled and any early symptoms of nitrogen narcosis I might experience. Once I was used to this depth he prepared me to dive deeper still. In the same way I had been fortunate with the quality of my diving instructors, I have also had wonderful instructors on land to support my understanding and development above the water. They showed me the importance of my belief system, the link between the outer and inner world and the benefits of being aware and heeding the signs given by both. They all emphasised the importance of self-acceptance and love.

Caroline Myss, in her audiobook *Archetypes: Who are You?* gives an interesting take on the importance of an inner dive. She explains that before the Second World War people were obsessed with discovering new lands; in more recent years, the focus has shifted to discovering who we are. Our internal world has become the new frontier. Many people have been awakened to a new impulse, compelling them to find and make sense of themselves. She believes this is essential for humanity and a necessary part of our evolution. Far from being an egotistic pastime, it is part of the transformation of humankind up the multisensory and multidimensional ladder. People are more willing to trust their intuitive responses. More people are becoming familiar with the idea that invisible does not mean a space is empty. Computers are helping to make this perception mainstream. Caroline Myss goes as far as to claim that in time people will refer to this era of technological data as "reptilian" and that humans, in the near future, will be accessing data in far more sophisticated ways.

Once we appreciate the power of the mind as a meaning-maker, able to interpret any given event as something personal and specific, we can reassess our assumptions. For example, when one stands out in a class or in a hall of school children and is told that they are different or that they need to be able to do more, it affects them on a deep level. I stood out in all the wrong ways at school and I made this experience mean there was something intrinsically wrong with me and that I was not good enough. Over time, such thought patterns create a meaning in your nervous system that becomes a feeling and a belief. This then develops into the lens through which you view and experience your world. Our beliefs become our reality as we look for more evidence to support such beliefs, dismissing the compliments and positive remarks we receive and claiming the negative ones. We therefore create further meaning that we are not enough, we don't fit in and we are not loved, resulting in unhappiness, but a sense that we are right. When we appreciate such beliefs are not necessarily true we can release them and replace them with ones that are more empowering and our experience starts to change.

## REFLECTION

The tide finally turned for me when I realised that if I believed other people had a right to exist and to be loved, then I must have that right as well. Later, through Melissa Sandon and her online Soul Leader's School, I again came to appreciate that if we are souls in human bodies how could we not believe we are worthy or be apologetic for our existence?

Although I have released many of the limiting stories I told myself, life continues to offer opportunities to support an ever deeper transformation. As mentioned earlier, my introduction to self-help came through Louise Hay, the Hay House Community and my Heal your Life® training with Dr. Patricia Crane. Before engaging in this work I was unaware that you could hide aspects of yourself as a means of protection. I also hadn't realised that during childhood we can shut down aspects of ourselves that seem to displease others and instead behave in ways that help us fit in. Inner child work was something I initially dismissed; I felt I did not need to go there. However, as I began to trust the process of inner reflection and the questioning of my beliefs, I revisited this strategy. It was certainly surprising to discover how much of what I heard as a child still plays a role in my thoughts and actions! This realisation led to the discovery of some interesting beliefs that needed to go. People seem to understand me now, or perhaps I have simply gained a better understanding of myself and thus communicate more clearly.

Another powerful insight was introduced to me by Kendall SummerHawk, a leader in the women's entrepreneurial movement and a strong advocate in the use of archetypes for self-discovery. Kendal SummerHawk points out that the way we do one thing in life is how we do many things. After all, on one level, everything is energy and hence responds similarly. It was fascinating to discover, through Kendall SummerHawk, that the same insights and responses that occur within you and your relationship to self could also be played out through, for instance, your relationship with money. This deeply resonated with me, as I had already come to understand how much of life is connected. I had previously learnt facial reflexology and was fascinated by the fact that, as with foot reflexology, parts of the face represent various parts of the body. My colour therapy course taught me the value of being aware of the energy of different colours, how this relates to our chakras and how they offer insights into what we crave emotionally and energetically. As with the mind-body connection and the belief that your body speaks your mind, there are insights everywhere and they provide lessons and opportunities to heal and change if you are prepared to look and take action.

Dr. Libby Weaver helped me become aware that our behaviour is the outer expression of our beliefs. When we create a meaning we merge it into facts, then take it forward into our life, not realising that it drives our behaviour. It stands to reason, then, that if you explore your beliefs you will come to understand what drives your behaviour. She encouraged me to appreciate why I do what I do, when I know what I know, especially when it comes to my health.

Up to that point, my body and mind had seemed ill-equipped for life on these shores. I felt as if, as Clarissa Pinkola Estes explains in her book, *Women who Run with the Wolves: Myths and Stories of the Wild Woman Archetype*, I had been trained to be maintained. That realisation does not sit well with your average mermaid! So I focused on feeling safer at being me; I began to accept the quirks and the idiosyncrasies. The reflections helped me see where I needed to make adjustments, including a good spring cleaning of all that didn't serve me. I focussed on my happiness. And, as so often happens when one makes adjustments in their own lives, my relationships with others changed as well.

## CASTAWAYS

Manta rays, the largest of which can be almost seven metres and weigh up to two tonnes, were there above me, hovering rather too close for comfort. I knew their status was vulnerable, but in that instant it was I who felt that way. Initially, I had been fascinated by the unique pattern of black spots on their underbelly. I had recently read how the Manta Trust was engaged in research and conservation projects and, as with whale sharks, photographs of their sightings are encouraged through online submission forms. Due to their unique markings manta rays can be identified and then tracked in the hope that we will learn more about these magnificent creatures. It had been a special moment, but any awe and wonder was quickly replaced by fear. I was not sure what they might do next. I was so close. I felt as if I were trapped in the light of a spaceship just before an alien abduction.

When they want to feed the manta rays uncurl their lobes to form paddle-like appendages. They then funnel the planktonic prey into their mouths where it is filtered from the water by sieve-like plates in the gills. I had just learnt about this before the dive and now it seemed I would experience it firsthand! I learnt later they had just been playing with my bubbles and any movement from me would have resulted in them darting away. My fear was just another mirror showing me that this was still a default mode. It gave me an opportunity to explore the stories I told myself in order to discern those that could be cast away and replaced by healthier ones.

I had come to realise that if mirrors were in all places, showing that how we do one thing is how we do most things, the real question becomes whether we desire change and if so, what, if anything, are we prepared to do to enact that change? This was made clear by that thirty-minute, up close and personal encounter with the manta rays that could have been totally magical, but for the worry over my survival. On diving deep again, I uncovered a story about mistrust, and some months later I had another chance to swim with them again. This time it was an incredible encounter.

I understood the importance of making space in my life for good to enter by clearing away, releasing and detoxing. I had cleared out cupboards and wardrobes, drawers and boxes, but I knew I would also need to clear away the old stories and corresponding beliefs that had kept me contained. With this process underway it was easier to make better choices all round, including what I ate and what I did with my time. Slowly, but surely, I started to trust my own inner voice again and by doing so, I noticed the conversations I received from others were more positive too.

I was also more vigilant about what I accepted. I learnt about healthy boundaries and the importance of not taking on the energy of others so easily. I learnt to appreciate the value of, as Sunny Dawn Johnston explained in her *11-Day Interactive and Experiential Intuition Camp*, being an *observer* rather than an *absorber*. I had enough stuff to get rid of without taking on someone else's!

## THE MERMAID'S TAIL

Through self reflection I came to realise I had mermaid tendencies within the mind and within the body. This meant I was able to use the mermaid metaphorically to support understanding and healing on both a physical and psychological level.

I am still flat-footed which, over time, resulted in tight leg muscles and pain in my lower back. When I also started to tire more easily, I realised there was some more diving to do. I had always considered myself healthy, but unhealthy habits slip in and the needs of the body change. This experience of malaise made me appreciate that, as well as focussing on the mind, the body also needs tender loving care. Sure enough, my adrenals were compromised and my gut and general digestive system was struggling. I allowed myself to imagine a healthier life. I wrote down all the qualities I hoped to reinstate and allowed myself to be open to new possibilities.

Dr. Libby Weaver was pivotal to my restorative journey and my present practice. Through her online presence she supported my fast track back to health. She rekindled my love of good food, helped me appreciate once more the importance of a healthy lifestyle, a relaxed digestive system and a stress-free perception. From this stance and feeling significantly better, I revisited Cheryl Richardson and the self-help programme outlined in her book, *The Art of Extreme Self-Care: Transform Your Life One Month at a Time,* which helped me secure positive and nurturing routines back into my life.

I came to appreciate that food and lifestyle choices are not all or nothing, wrong or right; rather, they are one decision after another. With each choice we have a chance to continue or choose again. It is the consistency of healthy choices made from informed decisions that light the way, while negative self-talk and judgement only depletes our resilience. Many of our daily habits determine the quality of our experiences and having beautiful rituals can make a big difference to the potential and sustainability to choose wisely and hence, influence our energy levels and ability to enjoy our life.

Later in life, I tried insoles for my shoes again. These were lighter and more discrete than the ones I'd had as a child. They also helped considerably; walking was more comfortable and I experienced less lower back pain. This in turn made physical activity more enjoyable, and I was able to shed ten kilos and return to the weight I was before I became, as Dr. Libby Weaver coined, "accidentally overweight."

Making the choice to support effective physical rejuvenation after lacking energy, being stiff and feeling uncomfortable is priceless. I now value my physical body and show it more respect than I had previously done. And while I may lack the sparkles of my mermaid tail, I do, on occasion, wear a sequined top!

## TREASURE

After experiencing this improvement, I wondered how I had been so complacent about my body for so long. But, as the saying goes, "When the student is ready the teacher appears." My teacher appeared as pain. I was aware that my body had been giving me signs for a long time which I had chosen to ignore. The signs got stronger and stronger until I, who had dived so deep into my psyche years before, now dived deep once more to uncover what was going on below the neck. Sometimes life takes hold and we change, little by little, until one day something inside of us seems to have disappeared. That energy and optimism, that drive and passion or the compassion and faith you had for the world seems to have waned. By diving deep once more you can discover that it has not gone, it has simply become hidden by layers of protection. Often, you just need to make some readjustments and healthy choices to reestablish your vitality again.

As I value myself more and appreciate, along with my spiritual side, the importance of a healthy mind and body, I make healthier choices more consistently. I also recently learnt the value of slower and gentler hobbies, such as sound healing, breath work and yoga, which support inner calm and flexibility. Mantras, mudras and time spent outdoors have also been powerful healing tools.

Appreciating the balance of life internally and externally allows you to appreciate the treasure of living your life.

## OUT OF THE BLUE

Life is often ironic and at times nonsensical. However, when you place more distance between yourself and such events you gain more clarity about the whats, whys and wherefores of your life.

Possibly one of the most painful periods of my life was my time in primary school. Having moved numerous times before and during my primary education, much of the continuity and progression of approach, as well as the content, was missing. This, coupled with what would now be assessed as having some type of special needs - language delay, dyslexia, attention deficit, dyspraxia, you name it and I probably had it - made learning and fitting in a challenge. These issues were further compounded by my being introverted with empathic tendencies.

The cosmic joke was that years later I ended up at school again, this time teaching the very age group that preceded the start of my unhappy experience. How and why I ended up back in the classroom comes down in part to the mystery of life. I also believe that because I was more aware of the delicate nature of young humans I could show them a level of compassion that would prevent the need for the same degree of healing I required. It was no coincidence, of course, that it was in that setting that I would receive my most significant healing. Through being with the children I came to see how magnificent their energy levels are, as well as their curiosity and their yearning to develop and gain skills. Most importantly, I witnessed their immense desire to engage fully with their world. This awoke my own desire to live fully. Later I went on to coach adults, especially those who had a hurt inner child.

Many opportunities, people and situations have appeared seemingly out of the blue, but on reflection they also answered some need in the most perfect of ways.

## CRYSTAL CLEAR

I am more appreciative of the benefit of being crystal clear about key hopes and desires I want to manifest. If you feel it, visualise it and believe it will happen, you can help its materialisation onto the Earth stage, especially when action accompanies such desire. There were also dreams I know I did not have for myself, but came through me nevertheless, and in divine timing.

I have gained greater understanding of the cycle of the waves and how they build up, crash and then slowly disperse. Yin and yang are important energies and understanding them helps my clarity of what part of the co-creation process I am operating within. For a successful and sustained flow there needs to be balance between the energies, although there is a time for both. There is a time for action, a time to receive and a time for rest, a time to dream and a time to celebrate. By enhancing my understanding of the consequences of the yin and yang energy, I am more deliberate in using the power of both of them.

## SURFING

Being more aware of my own energy levels and what recharges, maintains and depletes them has been beneficial. Knowing how to manage my energy enables me to socialise with others more successfully, enjoyably and with fewer unwanted repercussions. I value my daily rituals. I am more careful about the quality of my food, sleep and restorative routines. Having mermaid tendencies is not a reason for hiding away, but for making things happen and joining forces with others.

## THE MERMAID'S SONG

The mermaid's song is the message within the melody that exudes from your soul. It resonates with the frequency within you, stimulates your motivation and clarifies who you are. The mermaid's song invited me to explore my existence on a different wave. Her song plays in time with our own, arising from a quantum source where time and space interact and interface in different ways. The song offers an invitation to consider another way of operating, soothing the way for ourselves and all who have been before us. It supports us moving into the future in the way the first rockets moved into space, with excitement and hope, and because it was always inevitable.

## SEA-ING YOUR LIFE DIFFERENTLY

When I looked deeply and compassionately at the things I resisted, I found gifts to move my life forward. Resistance can hold you back, or it can be the reason for your growth. When you face resistance, consider:

- Why am I resisting this?
- Could I be operating from a default mode that is no longer an appropriate approach for me?
- Could fear be a strategy that no longer protects me?

## CREST OF A WAVE

When you appreciate the value of being alive, the experience of living becomes more precious. This chapter shared elements of my life and how I relate to the titles of the chapters in the hope it may shed further insights into your understanding of your own existence.

In chapter seven we explore the art of manifestation and the power of co-creation so the energy of success flows effortlessly with you, from you and to you. This reduces the need for you to do it all alone.

## MERMAID MINDSET

*By finding my resistance, I find an opportunity for treasure to flow.*

There are insights to be gained from exploring deeper into the reasons for resistance. Sometimes resistance is there for protection, real or perceived. Discerning between the two has been useful and has encouraged me to be far more adventurous with my life.

## MERMAID MOTTOS

Take time to consider some mermaid mottos. Feel free to use mine:

*I live courageously.*

*I allow myself to be.*

*I enjoy my life.*

## EXERCISE

GRATITUDE JOURNAL

I cannot overstate the importance of having gratitude for what you have in your life. If you can see what you have and appreciate it, you are in the vibration of attracting more of the same. There are times when it feels there is little to be grateful for, but if you want to shift your energy it is useful to flex the gratitude muscle. Like any muscle it has a memory and with use gratitude will become a more automatic response.

Your exercise for this chapter is to start a gratitude practice, to see through the eyes of appreciation and with a thankful heart. Give thanks each day for the things in your life you may take for granted. This process trains your mind to look for the positives rather than dwell on the negatives. For example, at the end of each day write in a journal:

*I am grateful for the food I ate today.*

*I am grateful for my friends that came to visit.*

*I am grateful for the promise of tomorrow.*

## SEA-C

## CONTRACT

If we acknowledge that we were born into our body, along with our soul, then the question of our life purpose becomes interesting. There is much debate about what we are here to *do*, but what if we are here just to *be*? Indeed, our ultimate task is to be ourselves, remove old beliefs and values that belong to others and reclaim our own essence. What we do with our being constantly changes as we chip away at the outer protection that smothers our soul.

- How would you behave if you knew you had made a contract with yourself and others to have an incredible life?

- How would you operate if you knew you were an essential piece in the puzzle of life?

- How would you act if you knew self-acceptance was an essential element in achieving your dreams?

# CHAPTER 6: TREASURE

*A space to journal my thoughts from this chapter…*

# A CONSIDERATION

What would make all the difference in your life? Why?

_____

_____

_____

If you were to talk to yourself at the age of six what would you say?

_____

_____

_____

If you were to give yourself advice in your teenage years what would it be?

_____

_____

_____

If you were to give yourself encouragement in your early adulthood what would you say?

_____

_____

_____

# COMMITMENT AND MY PLAN OF ACTION

Which of my many traits will I commit to valuing more today?

_____

_____

_____


What is my plan of action for uncovering more of my treasure?

_____

_____

_____

_____

_____

_____

_____

_____

_____

_____

_____

_____

_____

_____

_____

*I commit. Signed:* _____

# Chapter Seven

## OUT OF THE BLUE

*"I know about me. I am the moon's sister, a tidal child stranded on land. The sea always in my ear, a surf of eternal discontent in my blood."*

**— Keri Hulme**

## MERMAIDS LIVE OUT IN THE BLUE

**M**isunderstandings on land occur due to semantics and different world views. A deeper dive does not necessarily make the facts clearer, however, it does bring the realisation that our reality is not fixed, but moves gently and elusively. It is through our perception of time and our beliefs that opposing concepts can be simultaneously correct, incorrect and incomplete. Whilst we live with our filters on this physical plane, truth can seem as elusive as the source of strength within the seas, teasing you with growing understanding, but always keeping more out of sight in the great blue yonder. We live in a generation that has known space travel. Maybe we will also be the ones who will experience time travel and world peace. Such are the possibilities when you know anything can come out of the blue.

## A MOMENT IN TIME

The first time I saw the blue fluorescent plankton they mesmerised me. It was as if my mind could not believe what my eyes saw. The edge of the vibrant blue water seemed almost alive as it rippled and sparkled like the backdrop of an exclusive nightclub. I was told they were photo-luminescent. My friend, far more adventurous than me, ran straight into the sea shouting and laughing. She scooped up the blue in her hands, allowing it to splash down all around her. Some of it clung to her and made it look as if she was wearing a sequined top designed to impress. Within a few moments, daylight had commanded the space of dawn, and the fluorescent plankton had vanished. It was a miraculous experience, neither planned nor hoped for, as prior to this experience we had not even known of their existence.

For the mermaid, narrowing life down in order to manifest something specific and measurable is a challenge. They operate in the realm of the possible and live in the question. This cannot be easily defined or contained. A mermaid also feels the hopes of her sisters, past and present, and cannot always distinguish these from her own. Mermaids are more naturally guided to respond to life rather than demand from it. If you ask them to share their wish, it feels as if you have asked them to perform on stage, and you know how they feel about that!

I saw the blue plankton again, many years on during an early morning drift dive when the night had not yet faded into day. They shone miraculously. As I advanced closer they disappeared. I wondered what purpose their shine had. Did they shine for others or was it just for themselves? Did they feel admired and did they compare their glow to those nearby? As I saw more my spirit felt lifted. It was as if by seeing their shine, I could sense my own.

Mermaids seek to experience such sensations because they remember true joy. Within each mermaid is a calling to swim in love and to feel that total sense of completeness and peace again. The blue plankton came into my awareness unplanned, but with something special to offer. This encounter reminded me of the value of being open to the unexpected and to be in the moment in order to notice its arrival. Mermaids have made it their intention to be aware of the miraculous moments that can, if you let them, become your life.

For a mermaid to feel more land-operational it is useful to understand how the manifestation process works from both a place of miracle-mindedness and the magic of individual power.

## MANIFESTING MERMAIDS

You can feel out of place when those around you are goal-orientated and share their hopes and achievements with you, expecting you to share yours. For those with a mermaid energy it is a challenge to share your dreams and aspirations with others. Some have a hard time understanding your difficulty, as to them it seems like such a simple request.

The reasons are manifold. Mermaids are wired to prefer the manifestation process to unfold for them. Their role is to be available, to be aware and to allow. They are part of the global consciousness of shared love rather than the spirit of individual creation. Mermaids are also private by nature. This isn't necessarily about them not wanting to share, but about them not really knowing what answer to give and hence, preferring not to give any. They find it difficult to define who they are or what they want with a statement that doesn't allow for fluidity. For a mermaid in her shadow it is also about self-esteem; she feels, who am I to have a dream?

I felt as if I had struck gold many years ago when I came across the books of Marianne Williamson, a spiritual activist, author and lecturer. Her prose is beautiful, thought-provoking and inspiring. She discusses miracles and encourages her readers to ask open-ended questions to the Universe such as, "How can I be of service today?" or "What will you have me do?" These felt more open to the possibilities of the day than requesting expectations and the goal-orientated approach I had previously encountered. During my Heal Your Life® workshop we were encouraged to consider an area we wanted to improve in our lives, such as a better job, a beautiful home or enhanced fitness, then follow our request with, "I would like this or something better for my higher self." We were then to stand back and allow the Universe time and space to deliver.

My awareness was also expanded through the work of Dr. Dain Heer, renowned speaker, best-selling author and the co-creator of Access Consciousness. His approach is to live in the question and be open to the limitless possibilities of life. He encourages us to ask questions such as, "How does life get better than this?" Then go about your life in full expectation that you will be shown the answer.

Wishes are wonderful at times, but often you make a wish from a mindset that caused the situation that you want relief from. By purely wishing you make similar choices in the false hope that they will be your solution. Alternatively, you wish for something you think you want, only to discover when it arrives the joy it brings is fleeting. This happens either because you never really wanted it or because you are still in a place where you self-sabotage your dreams. Working with your inner mermaid helps to reduce the mismatch by aligning your true hopes and your inner vibration. It also helps you to be more open to miracles.

A good way of opening yourself up to miracles is increasing your awareness of what is happening within and around you. When you live with more awareness you are more in tune with the messages you give out and are given back. It is easier to see the signs and synchronicities and to respond to these opportunities accordingly. This is the mermaid's way.

When mermaids are in their flow they are miraculous at manifesting. They know the Universe supports them because they are part of the dance of creation. They respond as part of the Universe and not separately from it. Support an open, relaxed state of mind so you can be more in tune and raise your vibration through:

- Meditation, yoga or other mindful practices.
- A sport that allows you to be in the moment or encourages you to be reflective, such as gentle swimming.
- Walks and taking time in nature.
- Spending time with animals.
- Being with family and friends.
- Engaging in hobbies you like.
- Giving yourself permission to enjoy life.

## MIRACLE MINDEDNESS

I remember being at a marina preparing for a diving weekend and watching passengers climb aboard the other fun boats around us. Everyone seemed excited about the weekend escape. Some were carrying blow-up mermaid beds and others were wearing mermaid t-shirts and carrying glittery mermaid tails for that ultimate splash and photograph opportunity. Mermaid paraphernalia was everywhere and it seemed to transcend age. The young and the old appeared equally mesmerised by the idea of something miraculous, mystical and majestic. Maybe we all need an escape at times from the logic and confinement we have instilled into our world.

Mermaids understand that the majestic can be revealed at any moment. Indeed, how can you believe that what you see day-in and day-out are the only possibilities when you have been underwater and have witnessed creatures you didn't know shared your planet?

As mermaids are uncomfortable with labels as the ultimate definer, so too are they uncomfortable with being solely responsible for manifestation. Although mermaids know they dance with many labels simultaneously, such as, "I am a daughter, mother, wife and employee," they believe in the inclusive power of something that transcends the temporal and singular, preferring, "I am love." So it is with creation. It has always been a co-creation for them. It has always been about the totality and achieving for the higher good of us all.

Let's explore this miracle-mindedness approach to living so you can harness it in your own life.


## MYSTERY AS WELL AS MASTERY

The mermaid's approach to manifestation may appear less tangible than the goal-orientated manifestation process, but her results are just as impressive. She comes from a place of mystery, believing that life can line up to bring you what you had never expected, but perhaps always wanted on a deeper level.

The mermaid doesn't demand instructions and can find it confusing to be bombarded with measurable and goal-orientated information. She instead resides in a place of flow, where possibilities abound. She trusts and believes. She uses empathy and intuition and sees herself as part of a bigger picture, part of a whole, where life isn't about scarcity and about finite needs, but about enjoying the gifts of the Universe.

When you enter her space of mystery rather than mastery, you let life unfold. You know you can let things *be* rather than feel a need to *do* all the time. From this place of peace and calm, you allow inspirational thoughts to guide you in new directions. When you are open and in tune you know when you feel inspired and you sense when it is right to receive. Your emotions are your inner compass and they guide you well. Synchronicity abounds and you smile in appreciation when you reside in a Universe that, Gabrielle Bernstein, a motivational speaker, life coach and author coined, "has your back". People and opportunities come to you, so you don't need to take the metaphorical horse to water, the water comes to you.

Goals can be useful at times as you walk on land. They help steer your direction and keep you motivated in areas of your choosing. The mermaid is mindful that the world keeps evolving and everyone is finding their own way. She knows the student can gain more competencies than their master if the master feels that they have achieved all there is. She appreciates that life is a journey of experiences rather than a vehicle to a destination. The mermaid knows she is not the master. She encompasses the mystery of being, for she believes in spiritual alchemy.

## GUIDANCE AS WELL AS A GATEWAY

The way of the mermaid is not to present a gateway through which to enter. What the mermaid offers is guidance; an awareness of our own internal and external communication channels. Hence, it is important to relax the mind and become aware of our visions, imagination and where our attention is drawn.

The journey to a miraculous life is knowing that life is supporting you with one synchronistic event after the next. The mermaid appreciates that we are at different points on our journey and that before we become effortless in our miracle-mindedness we need to feel light of spirit. Our heavy loads are best left behind. This leaves space and energy to enjoy the moment and to move into the future with more ease.

Mermaids won't invite you to queue at the same gate with others. You are here to be part of the creative expansive Universe that pulsates, in ever-increasing outward circles, while simultaneously creating new portals.

## MESSAGES RATHER THAN A MISSION

Mermaids see the signs and respond to messages. In their flow they know when to come close and when to keep their distance. They understand when they can respond by themselves, when help is necessary and when helping others is the only way forward. Life is love in action and the action can be enjoyed when it comes from a place of compassion and trust. Our purpose is not to survive our life, but rather to live it to the fullest and to radiate our brightness that is part of the inter-connectedness of the light. We can achieve much together if the participants come willingly and are truly allowed to contribute to a shared aim, rather than having to contain their true selves to fit in to something that could be so much better.

Mermaids know that they live in an expanding Universe where what was appropriate today may be irrelevant tomorrow. Our part is to flow with the change and to see the messages about where we are needed, rather than continue with a mission that, with the passing of time, is no longer appropriate.

## SAGE RATHER THAN AGE

Mermaids are ageless as they encompass all ages. They have the curiosity of a child and the wisdom of a sage.

When we are not in our flow we experience resistance. Labels such as age can contain pre-conceived judgements rather than empowering us with insights. It is what we gain through experiencing that matters. We have many examples of the young achieving outstanding feats and older people defying what is expected of their age. Mermaids are here to continue to stretch the boundaries. With the sage comes the wisdom and with the youth comes the curiosity and drive to entertain possibilities.

When these qualities are combined there is a greater awareness of when to do something and when to stand or hold back. There is less inner struggle and more time to appreciate the beauty and the innate intelligence of life itself. There is a desire to sustain such an existence. There is time to be curious about new possibilities rather than leaping immediately into action, unless it feels right to do so. There is peace in appreciating who you are and your place in the Universe.

## THE MERMAID RESURFACES

Much has been written about manifestation. The mermaid resurfaces to redress the balance that we don't always need to control the process of life and navigate ourselves to some specific location. The mermaid surrenders, but with integrity. She doesn't accept everything, but drawers to her the rewards of being present and in alignment with her purpose. We need to hold a space for miracles. By doing so we can find ourselves somewhere spectacular, having supported others on the way.

## SEA-ING YOUR LIFE DIFFERENTLY

Life appears easier if you know what you want and use the law of attraction effectively. However, this is not the only way, and it is not the way of the mermaid. The boundaries of what's possible do not need to be confined by your present thinking.

How would your day unfold if you knew that life would take care of you and that you lived in a loving Universe? As you go about your day, be mindful. Bring your awareness to the different ways the world communicates with you.

- Notice the songs and the message they share.
- Notice the conversations around you as you wait your turn in a queue.
- Look for repetition in number signs and seek understanding of what such numbers mean.
- Home in on your own emotions and gut reactions.
- Be mindful of your energy levels.
- Stay open to possibilities.

## CREST OF A WAVE

When you are the captain of your own ship you navigate to where you want to go. When you trust the universal laws of nature and go with the flow, you go where you have never been before.

This chapter looked at the limitations of approaching the manifestation process from an individual standpoint only, rather than from a place of openness and miracle-mindedness. The idea of miracles occurring out of the blue, by the Universe presenting synchronistic events to guide you, is in itself a miraculous concept to entertain.

There are benefits to manifesting from a personal viewpoint. Chapter eight explores the manifestation process from this stance and offers some more mermaid twists.

## MERMAID MINDSET

*I let things be and I make things happen.*

The mermaid allows her imagination to soar and is inspired by all that makes her sing. There is a time to make things happen, as there is a time to let things be. The mermaid mindset is prepared to trust and allow the miracles of the Universe to unfold.

I was driven for much of my life. I focussed so hard on trying to realise my goals that I missed out on some of the journey and on the experience of being in the moment. I now appreciate that there are different ways to get to the same destination and many are more interesting and easier than the ways I choose for myself. Goals are important, but so is trusting in the Universe and allowing miracles into your everyday moments - the unplanned and the unexpected. Such moments come out of the blue and take you into the blue, offering exciting possibilities and resulting in perfect moments.

## MERMAID MOTTOS

Before you journal, write some mermaid mottos to uplift you.

*I believe in miracles and I experience them all the time.*

*I trust the Universe knows the right channels for me and I love where they flow.*

*I am amazed at what I experience when I resist less and allow more.*

## EXERCISE

Some will argue it was a coincidence that you saw a dolphin after you asked to see such a dolphin as evidence of the Universe communicating with you. Others know this is synchronicity.

SYNCHRONICITY

Take time in your day to slow down. Become mindful of what you are doing and sensing. Reflect on, and notice, synchronistic events that you may have previously thought were coincidences. Ask to see a specific sign and notice when you do.

## SEA-C

CO-CREATE

When you are in the energy of co-creation you take what has never been before and make it possible. You give it form. Implicit in your co-creation is something special and unique for humanity.

*When I am open to all that is possible I create more than I could possibly imagine.*

# CHAPTER 7: OUT OF THE BLUE

*A space to journal my thoughts from this chapter…*

_____

_____

_____

_____

_____

_____

_____

_____

_____

_____

_____

_____

_____

_____

_____

_____

_____

_____

_____

_____

_____

_____

# A CONSIDERATION

Where can you let go and let it be in your life?

_____

_____

_____

Where are you struggling in life to maintain control?

_____

_____

_____

Reflect on what in your life came out of the blue?

_____

_____

_____

How will you use your imagination today?

_____

_____

_____

# COMMITMENT AND MY PLAN OF ACTION

What sign will I commit to noticing today that will encourage my awareness of synchronistic events?

_____

_____

_____


What is my plan of action for incorporating the mermaid's way into my life?

_____

_____

_____

_____

_____

_____

_____

_____

_____

_____

_____

_____

_____

*I commit. Signed:* _____

# Chapter Eight

## CRYSTAL CLEAR

*"If the private life of the sea could ever be transposed onto paper, it would talk not about rivers or rain or glaciers or of molecules of oxygen and hydrogen, but of the millions of encounters its waters have shared with creatures of another nature."*

— **Federico Chini**, ***The Sea of Forgotten Memories***

## CRYSTAL CLEAR ABOUT MERMAIDS

Manifesting mermaids operate in the moment, yet in deep alignment with their authentic self and their mission, both of which are timeless. Their manifesting is successful as it is the consequence of knowing who they are and what they want, after clearing away the smudges on the family jewels. Mermaids in their flow are crystal clear about when to create and when to let it be. There is a time for the yin energy of receiving, either by letting things come to you or you flowing effortlessly to them. There are also times when the direct action of the yang energy is required to support the process of transforming dreams into reality.

## MILLIONAIRE MERMAIDS

There are some dives when you cannot believe your eyes. You feel as if you are swimming in a dream. The intensity and variety of colours and shapes moving around you almost defy your senses. You feel part of the scene as well as a spectator, and you bathe, calm and serene, in the wonder of it all. Surrounded by such variety and exuberance, your eyes hardly know where to feast. When you interact with nature you feel an increase in contentment and relaxation. Research by a national marine aquarium found that visitors had a reduction in their heart rates and blood pressure after watching the marine life. No surprise then that my buddy and I always feel relaxed and revived after a diving trip.

A mermaid in her element is abundant beyond our wildest dreams. She flows freely between all she sees with grace and ease, supporting those she encounters on her way. All she requires materialises before she has finished her request, so in tune is she with her world and her place within it. This is her natural state as she flows with life, vibrating at a high frequency and radiating out appreciation, gratitude and trust.

On Earth we have dreams and desires and some people manifest seamlessly. There are some amazing entrepreneurs that are manifesting magnificent lives for themselves. I am sure many of you would like some of that as well, and why not? Think of all the ways you could help yourself and others if you were a millionaire mermaid!

Inspired by a movement of female entrepreneurs, empowered in their business and passionate in their desire to help others, let's uncover the millionaire secret to accelerated manifestation using the law of attraction with a mermaid's twist.

## MANIFESTING WITH THE WAVES OF LIFE

We are all children of the Universe with dreams that we came into this world to realise. However, for some people, the dreams seem impossible to achieve and the beauty of life is lost for a while. When you begin to appreciate and understand your inner programming you can start to reclaim power over your life experiences again. You can quieten the inner voice that tells you that you can't do things. You can replace such negative sentiments with more empowering ones like "I can try again!" The tools and strategies mentioned in this book can help you shake off the heavy cloak of negativity you may wear, leaving you free to choose another way. The Universe is waiting for you to play.

There is a space through which you can travel where the gentle souls and dreamers dwell, to share their vision for a better world. Together they turn their visions into our new reality.

*"If you could be anything you wanted," said the mermaid, "choose to be you!"*

## 1.  SEA/E CLEARLY

Seeing clearly is twofold. It means being clear about what you wish to manifest and also being clear about any blocks within you interfering with its materialisation.

Manifestation is an incredible tool. It is working for you all the time, though many do not appreciate this or understand that their vibration level matters. Your thoughts and fears are given the same attention as your hopes and dreams. It is therefore important to appreciate what you are thinking and feeling as these contribute to your vibrational point of attraction. If your hopes are not in alignment with them it will impact the ease and flow of their arrival. If you believe the process doesn't work, that will be your experience.

Being aware of your own perception needs emphasising so you can appreciate the importance of it in the manifestation process. The lens through which you view your world will colour your experience of it. Being aware of this places you in a better position to witness your inconsistency. Consequently, you can then be more conscious about what you are thinking and doing so you can have more alignment with the experiences you desire.

If you hope to be a successful singer, but hold the belief that you never get lucky breaks and you'd be no good on stage, you can see how your hopes and beliefs are in conflict. In other words, your beliefs are undermining your ability to manifest. Your fears will be manifested instead as they are the stronger and more consistent vibrational match. If you do manifest a singing opportunity, there is a strong chance that you will sabotage it or at least place a ceiling on how successful you will be. This is why it is important to dive deep and start a compassionate communication with your inner mermaid to uncover your subconscious programming and potential blocks to your conscious dreams.

When first practicing manifestation, you want to play with the energy of creation so that you gain confidence that it works. Start by manifesting small, every day desires that can be requested clearly and witnessed almost instantly, for example, finding a parking place, gaining a seat on the bus or being able to make a reservation at a restaurant that is usually booked solid. Notice the dopamine high when your desire materialises and use this state of positivity to request more. As you continue to flex and strengthen the manifesting muscle, pay close attention to your focus. Is it on what has worked or what has not? Once you get used to asking for simple requests and expecting positive results, consider more expansive and longer-term goals. Remember to be crystal clear about these goals. I remember one humorous story shared by a fellow workshop attendee about her hoped intention of being surrounded by money, only to find herself working in a bank!

Abundance is an energy and it flows with joy. There are times when you hope to manifest, for instance, more money, when in fact it is the freedom to travel that would be the source of your joy. In this case, any good feeling resulting from an increase in salary would be short-lived if you remain in your job and are still unable to travel. It is therefore helpful to reflect on what you really want to experience and why. Being crystal clear about what you wish to feel, do, be and have will support your ability to manifest more successfully. It is important to know what your success criteria is, so you can recognise when you have been successful.

What do you want more of and what will be the consequence for you? These ideas can help you home in on some of the abundance you want to experience:

- Freedom

- Health

- Self-worth

- Fulfilment

- Time

- Respect

- Faith

- Joy

- Love

- Peace

Consider:

- Expecting positive outcomes. Many of us regularly expect the worst.

- Manifesting consciously and on a regular basis. We manifest unconsciously all the time.

- Consistently using strategies and tools to support a positive inner environment from where new dreams arise.


## 2.   TIDAL LAWS

The law of attraction requires key elements to be in place, so it can work for you. These include gratitude for your life and faith in the manifestation process. They influence your vibration and become the frequency that is attracted back to you.

As previously mentioned, what you believe matters. If there is friction between your hopes and your inner beliefs, the stronger will be the point of attraction. If you believe manifestation doesn't work, you will find the evidence so it becomes your self-fulfilling prophecy. If you believe in it, or are willing to believe in it, and celebrate when you see it in action, your awareness will more naturally flow towards success.

It can be difficult to take action before you have trust. The paradox is that you must sometimes step out in faith and take action in order to support the process. Once you start taking those deliberate first few steps, however small they may be, you tell the Universe you believe and change starts to occur. It's not the other way round.

If you wake up in a bad mood, notice how the traffic lights all seem to be red and the traffic appears slower. You feel your bad day is getting worse as you now think that you are going to be late. You can continue with these negative thoughts - namely, that the world is against you - or you can shift them. Declare that you will get safely to your destination and focus your attention on something you are grateful for. The combination of the two can start to raise the low vibration you awoke with. Then notice how life seems to flow better for you when you feel more content. When you have positive energy it radiates from you, just as negativity does when you are in a bad mood. Who would you prefer to be with, someone exuding positivity, or the opposite?

With some requests we need to exercise patience because these laws work in their own timeframe, not ours. This timeframe is often referred to as "divine timing." If we allow doubt and a lack of trust to enter our minds we interfere with the energy and hold our desire at arm's length.

It is important to have space in your life for a new dream to take form. If you are still holding on to everything tightly, you can see how this sends a conflicting message about wanting something new. People have often shared that it was only after they had removed the last of their ex-partner's possessions from their house that they found a new love. It was only when they forgave their previous boss for perceived unfairness that their perfect career path materialised. Life moves forward when there is contentment for your present state.

Notice what you are grateful for and what you take for granted. If you find a coin on the ground do you pick it up and believe it is a sign that more is on its way, or do you feel disgruntled that it's such a small amount? The Universe works with the vibration of appreciation. Get excited as you give thanks for the good in your life and as you imagine more happening. Consider:

- Listening to inspiring people who have turned their lives around. Use this as motivation for you to believe, instead of judging yourself with comparisons.

- Joining organisations that share the messages you want to hear. Tap in to positive Facebook posts, join a MeetUp group, and explore the numerous websites and communities that share uplifting ideas and self-development messages.

## 3. GO WITH THE FLOW

This part of the manifestation process is about the importance of going with the flow of life. This is not about blindly floating along, but about noticing the signs and acting on them. It is about being fully in the moment and being aware of what is happening within and around you. Being fully present enables you to play your part in the co-creation process and to be aware of your uniqueness in what gives you joy and what joy you can give to others.

When you are in your flow you notice the change in currents and the choices ahead to move towards the right or left. You move with the current, but not purely at its mercy. Be mindful of self-doubt and negative self–talk, and choose instead to stay steadfast in your passion, focus and commitment, acknowledging the part you play in your own experience. Denise Duffield-Thomas advocates using anchors as part of our routine to keep a positive focus on our dreams. For example, she places positive messages in her calendar that regularly pop up on her phone and computer. She changes her passwords so that they are the goals she wants to achieve. Keep positive about the manifestation of your dreams and consider the use of:

- Affirmations and "I am" statements

- Vision boards

- Visualisation

- Gratitude journals

This is manifesting the mermaid's way.

## 4. RIDING THE WAVE

Life is about contraction and expansion, the ebb and the flow. It is also about the unification of our body and our soul. The mermaid can feel when it is time to go with the flow, when to ride the waves and when to take stock. Part of the manifestation process, as mentioned previously, is knowing about the energy of life and appreciating there is a time for all things. A wave builds up momentum, under the water as well as above, before it reaches its peak and comes crashing down, slowing its pace before the cycle starts again. This section is about being mindful about where you are in the manifestation process. Are things being created in divine timing below the surface, or is it time for you to take action? As the wave slows down, this is the time to appreciate the ride and to reflect on events. It's also a good time to consider what engagement you may want with the next wave.

Considering where you are in the manifestation process gives you a better appreciation of how best to respond, be it with patience, reflection, enjoyment or action.

Some of us are in the midst of prolific transformation, whilst others may be allowing it bit by bit; still others are just entertaining the idea of change. All positions are to be applauded. This is your journey, and it will play out in its own unique way. Learn from others and let them be an inspiration, but don't give your power away through comparisons that undermine your aim, or try to copy them by swimming their channel without their current. You have your own wave to ride!

## HIGH WATERS

If something you hoped for doesn't seem to be materialising, think about where in the process you are as well as where there might be a conflict of intention. There are times you will be in the energy of expansion and at other times contraction. Keep the faith and be willing to see synchronicity everywhere to help you with your next response.

You may plateau in your success rate and if you do, reflect on the process again. Although this manifestation process is written in a linear way, it intermingles with many elements being played out simultaneously and so your original hopes change and are replaced by new ones. If you feel your life is not moving for you, reflect on each section again. Is it really what you want? Contemplate what belief is not serving you that either sneaked back in or you had not previously been aware of.

If the process doesn't seem to be working pause and review. Consider:

- Am I being patient enough?
- Am I seeing and actioning the signs that are presented to me?
- Am I consistent with my positive thought patterns and beliefs?
- Could I be self-sabotaging and if so, where could this be?
- What is my upper limit and do I need to remove resistance to raise it again?
- Am I in a cycle of expansion or contraction?
- Have I left space for a miracle or am I being too controlling?
- Is my desire for my highest good?
- Was I crystal clear about my goal?
- Do I appreciate the progress I've made?

Continue to engage with your inner mermaid. She may well hold the keys to your dreams, so make sure she hasn't locked the treasure box and darted off with them!

## SEA-ING YOUR LIFE DIFFERENTLY

What if life was more a co-creation than you had previously realised? How would you change if you felt more empowered and knew your choices were important?

• Where could you start taking more responsibility for your daily experiences?

• If it is important to maintain a high vibration, what changes can you instigate to support this?

• If you wake up feeling negative, how could you turn this around?

When we realise our power, we can make empowered decisions.

## CREST OF A WAVE

This chapter uncovered the tools of the abundant mermaid, exploring how best to manifest.

The next chapter discusses the importance to the mermaid of finding her sisters rather than swimming the seas alone.

## MERMAID MINDSET

*I dive deep so I can enjoy the shallow.*

By diving deep you can start to appreciate life more. You realise it's about making the most of everyday moments with the people that are precious to you. It is about having and spreading your happiness.

In the past, I was not in the habit of asking or accepting support from other people or from the Universe. I hadn't realised how controlling I was, or that I was closed to many possibilities because of fear, which I hid behind a cloak called "independence". With time and practice, however, I became more extravagant with my requests and more enthusiastic in my acceptance and discovered it was a win-win for me and for those around me.


## MERMAID MOTTOS

Before you journal, reflect on some mermaid mottos to keep you motivated. You are welcome to swim with mine.

*I believe in the manifestation process.*

*I am a manifesting mermaid.*

*I am worthy of abundance.*


## EXERCISE

HEALTHY HABITS, RITUALS AND ONGOING ANCHORS

You are a powerful being. You have a strong muscle memory that seems to automatically reset to previous patterns if you are not mindful. If you desire substantial change you need to fully embed it by creating new positive habits, routines and rituals and sticking with them until this way of being becomes your new automatic.

To keep your resolve alive, set reminders for yourself. For example, if your hope is for a new job, write, "I love my new job" on cards and place them in your home where you will see them on a daily basis. You can place a mermaid motto in your phone that flashes your goal, such as your ultimate weight loss, on a daily basis. You can create a vision board that is uplifting to see, showing next year's holiday destination, as well as placing positive statements on your computer or in your diary. Your daily gratitude journal will also keep you on track and listening to positive songs can keep your vibration high.

## SEA-C

CONSISTENCY AND CLARITY

When you are more consciously aware of what you are doing you can be more conscious about doing what you want. Through clarity you are better placed to co-create with life, and through consistency you are better placed to turn dreams from something imagined into something real.

*I am crystal clear and consistent in my intentions for a better life.*

# CHAPTER 8: CRYSTAL CLEAR

*A space to journal my thoughts from this chapter…*

_____
_____
_____
_____
_____
_____
_____
_____
_____
_____
_____
_____
_____
_____
_____
_____
_____
_____
_____
_____
_____
_____
_____
_____

# A CONSIDERATION

What do you want to experience more of and why?

_____

_____

_____

Have you discovered a counter-belief to your intended manifestation?

_____

_____

_____

What insights have you gained about yourself and your desires for manifestation, and what are the ramifications of these?

_____

_____

_____

What could you do to ensure consistency of action for your intended change?

_____

_____

_____

# COMMITMENT AND MY PLAN OF ACTION

What crystal clear anchor will I commit to placing in my life today?

_____

_____

_____

What is my plan of action for manifesting one of my desires?

_____

_____

_____

_____

_____

_____

_____

_____

_____

_____

_____

_____

_____

_____

*I commit. Signed:* _____

# Chapter Nine

## SURFING

*"We are like islands in the sea, separate on the surface but connected in the deep."*

**— William James**

## SURFING MERMAIDS

**M**ermaids hold the portal between two realities: that of the sea and that of the land. When they're in their flow they ride the crest of the waves in harmony and joy with their sisters, living, nurturing and appreciating life. When mermaids are in their flow they find where they belong and where they are needed. When the sisters work together they support humanity to once again vibrate in harmony with the Earth-Song.

## IMMERSION TO EMERGENCE

Everyone is vital to the tapestry of life. Mermaids play their part in a wider conversation about temperament. Our planet requires creative and deep thinkers to address the polarisation of our world's issues. People are beginning to realise that we have a cultural bias towards extroversion which is causing an imbalance in how we operate as a society. Being loud isn't always the best way and it certainly isn't the only way. There are benefits to listening to other possibilities regarding our approach to current issues. As a society we could be heading towards the rocks, having shunned the ones that could save us. If we don't address this imbalance we will all struggle. We all benefit from the empowerment and validation of planet Earth's inhabitants.

From an individualistic viewpoint, disowning who you are can make you sick. From a societal viewpoint it results in the above-mentioned bias or imbalance. We know even a slight imbalance from the usual temperature of the sand can result in the potential distinction of the turtle, as the heat during gestation determines the gender of the egg. The result of a go-getter-biased society is there may not be anything left to go-get.

This is the time for the mermaids to heal, personally and collectively. Through the mermaids' healing they also soothe ancestral unrest, aiding the potential for collaboration once more.

*"The importance isn't the splash I make when diving into the water, beautiful one, it's the energy shift you make by diving fully into your life on land!" exclaimed the mermaid.*

## MERMAID REVIVAL

About thirty devil rays swam by. Were they in a definite formation? They sped by so fast it was unclear whether there was a leader, or if the front position was exchangeable. I remember tucking the question away to research, which I did later that week. It resulted in a chance encounter with a website, followed by a deliberate search for a TED talk, which precipitated my in-depth research into introversion and developed my understanding and appreciation of different temperaments. I quickly realised I had discovered something valuable.

It was Susan Cain who stirred the waters for me with her book, *Quiet: The Power of Introverts in a World That Can't Stop Talking*. She is also the chief revolutionary and co-founder of Quiet Revolution and campaigns for changes at work and in educational establishments. She explains that these places are more geared towards extroverts who excel at being bold, alpha, and gregarious. Susan Cain explains, through data, research and stories, that these favoured traits are now part of our definition of leadership and our assumptions about what good performance looks like. She is clear about the dangers of this bias which marginalise the many strengths that the quieter souls have regarding the creative process and problem-solving in the workplace and in society. She encourages us to appreciate, once again, the importance to society of character over personality.

The mermaid revival is happening one ripple after another and one deep dive after the next. The tipping point has passed and there is a greater awareness of the benefits of a quieter disposition and the harm of shaming people for being different. The second of January 2011 saw the first World Introvert Day and although this isn't an official holiday, it is celebrated around the world. The event is twofold; in addition to giving introverts the chance to recharge after the festive holidays, it also promotes awareness of the strengths of a quieter and more reflective nature in the hope that this will reduce the damaging labels often placed on them.

## CONNECTIVITY

I met a diver on holiday. She was passionate about conservation, but she was also pragmatic. She was happy to talk about what was going on, what has gone on and the consequences of continuing as we are. It all seemed alarming. She talked about the possibility of a positive future if deliberate action was taken by the world's inhabitants and if it became a political decision to ensure ocean conservation was a priority and an overriding first choice. She was realistic and hopeful. She believes each of us has a part to play, some through day to day activities, others through lobbying for change on a larger scale. She explained how we are interlinked and that the sea provides a sig-nificant proportion of the oxygen we need. She talked about pollution and how, with the tides and currents, pollutants move miles from the offending individual or country. The night before, we had seen the video of the turtle's stomach full of plastic. This encouraged us to heed her words and do what we can to make changes, strengthening the tide, to ensure the sustainability of our existence on the planet.

We spent several evenings talking about marine life and the amazing, mutually beneficial interconnection between different organisms, as well as the vulnerability of the eco-system to even the slightest variation. This dive instructor was travelling the world, studying marine life and the environment, collecting data in order to share and inform others. She opened up a world of possibilities and emphasised the need to take action now. Her work did not bring with it an impressive pension, quality conditions of service or a high salary. What she was concerned about was promoting action in others in order to support sustainable seas; a healthy legacy that this generation can leave for the next. This is priceless.

There are different types of relationships and different ways that species operate to ensure their survival, from parasitic to symbiotic. As I looked ahead of me during one dive, I saw a lone turtle swimming slowly in an upward direction. I wondered if it had a mate. I knew its future was in jeopardy and strongly hoped this would not prove to be the case.


## PLENTY OF FISH IN THE SEA

Darwin's survival of the fittest theory contributed greatly to our understanding of the dynamics of life. The destruction to our eco-system by companies, countries and individuals trying to get ahead and to succeed at all cost, now begs the question, "How long can this approach last?" There is a growing realisation that for the sake of humanity there needs to be a different way from the cut-throat idea of bigger, better, stronger and faster.

Mermaids understand the eco-system and the benefits of working with it and not against it. Under the water there are many examples of how species collaborate rather than merely fighting for their right to survive. Clownfish or nimo fish are coated with a layer of mucus that protects them from the poison of the anemones' tentacles where they swim. Both the anemones and the clownfish benefit. The fish help clean the anemones, provide nutrients in the form of waste and scare away predatory fish. The nimo fish in return gets to reside in the safety of the tentacles that are poisonous to others.

In the end, if there are no fish in the sea, no one wins.

## SEA OF CREATIVITY

Mermaids know that as mermaids they are perfect; on land, however, many feel anything but. It seems like they are spending their entire lives trying to accept themselves and to integrate the different parts into a whole. Bridging the two worlds so you feel in alignment with who you are is hard enough, but when this is accompanied by a cultural distain for your natural disposition it is not surprising that many swim off by themselves.

Many mermaids don't have the confidence of their sisters who were born to sit on their Earth throne. They don't have the natural disposition to command an audience and feel their authenticity radiate with a charismatic effect. They are part of the sea. They radiate at a different frequency, so easily hurt and so easily bruised. But now the goddesses are standing by their thrones and are reaching down to take the hands of their sisters. There is no competition. The goddesses know the mermaids are an essential piece of the puzzle for the world's salvation. Do we continue in this age of polarisation, with its competition and win-lose scenarios, or do we enter an age of balance and harmony with co-creation, contribution and compassion as its cornerstones? If we choose the latter we can embrace vulnerability, which, when coupled with courage, allows a sea of creativity to be valued. The divine feminine in us all understands that the desire for conflict and competition needs to be put to rest if we wish to move forward into the landscape of nurturing, protection, contribution and sustainability.

The sisters are in alignment. They know that the receptivity of the feminine yin needs the balance of the masculine energy of decision making and action taking. The healthy and abundant mermaid is essential for the continued evolution of humanity. Their mission on land is to spread the message that the sea needs our help if it is to continue to be our bloodline. To support its harmonic rhythm we help it by clearing our own polluted thoughts.

If the mermaid is not empowered she will help no one, but will remain hidden like the spaghetti-eels that disappear into the sand flats at the first sign of disturbance. When she is in her right channel she is unstoppable, moving and contributing to the creative currents of the seas.

## AYE, AYE CAPTAIN

In support of her mission to restore balance and harmony in our lives the mermaid has joined forces with her goddess sisters so together they can claim their seats as the captains of their destiny. There comes a time when we need to appreciate the importance of taking responsibility for steering ourselves through the currents of life. We can take command of our own journey, but also the future of those to come. The sisterhood is contributing to a societal change by ensuring that collaboration and creativity are valued and that competition is not at the expense of human survival. Mermaids can highlight the consequences of continuing as we are, as well as offer coordinates to bring us back on track. Without the mermaids in place, who will save the metaphorical boats from their inevitable crash against the rocks?

## BLUE OCEAN PERSPECTIVE

Mermaids respond better when they are not in competition, but rather in collaboration.

Mermaids who are comfortable with their own identity are taking the stage and demonstrating a different way of operating in business. They are independent, successful and entrepreneurial. They are motivated by a desire to help others and they understand the manifestation process of miracles and magic. They are shining a new light on the way business can operate through collaboration and compassion. Once you are in alignment with who you are, you vibrate at the frequency of miracles. Once you are at peace with yourself, you are better placed to enable others. Indeed, you become more aware of the connection between us all and notice the beautiful dance of how helping others results in being helped yourself. The sisters in their divine feminine are holding the light together.

Marie Forleo, the highly successful life coach, speaker and philanthropist, is an example of this new way. Marie describes herself as a "multi-passionate entrepreneur", for rather than focussing on one aspect of a business, she engages in a range of activities that include being an author, the host of her own TV show, creating coaching programmes, and so forth. She is not alone in her approach. More and more people are appreciating and spreading the word that the world is not defined as it was before. It is wide open and unexplored and so much is possible if we are prepared to imagine and believe.

In their books, *Blue Ocean Strategy: How to Create Uncontested Market Space and Make Competition Irrelevant* and *Blue Ocean Shift: Beyond Competing - Proven Steps to Inspire Confidence and Seize New Growth* and *Blue Ocean Leadership*, W. Chan Kim and Renee Mauborgne describe how some of the most successful companies are focussed not on displacing existing businesses, but developing new markets that weren't there before. These authors are playing their part in developing a new language to describe what is happening, and I love the analogy between the blue ocean and a vast, unexplored marketplace, where the future is not about destruction, but expansion.

## CHANGING THE FREQUENCY AND WAVES ONLINE

One need only scan websites and blog feeds to see that something exciting is taking place. The internet is being used by many people with a mission to help others realise their dreams and to make a positive contribution to the world.

Susan Cain is one of a growing number of gentle souls who is providing a safe place online to support open-minded individuals. She is inclusive, inviting men and women, introverts, extroverts and ambiverts who believe in the power of complementary personality styles to become involved. Her call to action is for people to be ambassadors for change, spreading the value and importance of communities coming together to, "leverage the strengths of both introverts and extroverts resulting in workplace cultures where no potential remains untapped or under-appreciated." Beth Buelow, founder of The Introvert Entrepreneur in 2010, also has the aim of providing a safe space where introverts can gain insight and support. She encourages empowerment, entrepreneurship and leadership by embracing their qualities.

The world becomes a better place when individuals utilise their power of collaborative creation while simultaneously realising their soul contract, which is connected intrinsically to the development of others. When a woman has struggled in her depths, but negotiated turbulent currents and survived, she appreciates the beauty of life and wants others to have the chance to experience it too.

## THE MERMAID MOMENTUM

Many people believe that a group of people with a common goal have more chance of success than those who focus on the goal alone. Mermaids may well start out alone, but as confidence and belief in what they do develops, circumstances lead them to other like-minded people. The alchemy of the sisterhood is something to behold. A group that supports your individual success while at the same time striving for a common goal achieves miraculous results. Under-pinning this success is a belief that unless we all win, none of us wins, rather than the limited belief that if you win, there is less of a chance that I will.

We have heard of the power of prayer and here in the deep waters the mermaids sing again, telling anyone who listens of the importance of the sisterhood for our survival.

As mentioned earlier, Marianne Williamson has been one of my greatest teachers. In one of her talks, she said that the health of a nation can be measured by how it treats its female population and how the female population is empowered to ensure the protection of their community. Marianne Williamson indicated that the two were linked, and to underestimate this could be ultimately disastrous for harmonious living. There are times you can feel the tears of the mermaids as they cry and lament over the pain of their sisters on land - the gendercide, abuse and general lack of compassion between one human and another. Marianne Williamson advocates strongly that this is no time for women to be asleep. She explains that the world needs them to act in protection of their family in the widest possible sense.

There is something spectacular happening on planet Earth. There is more information, more opportunities and more encouragement than ever to become involved. The level at which you hope or wish to engage is your choice. The mermaid celebrates the little wins as well as the big ones. She applauds miraculous thinking and faith in the infinite over limitation. As Marianne Williamson explains, faith isn't blind, it's visionary. The mermaid envisions peace on land.

## REWIREMENT NOT RETIREMENT

Throughout this book I have emphasised that the mermaid, though she embodies the wisdom of the sage, is ageless. Indeed, what we are seeing in the wider community is women of all ages riding their waves with increasing success. Those that may have retired are relishing the opportunities to liberate themselves and are enjoying the transformation of midlife, accelerating the level of their own empowerment and supporting it in others. The young are also taking the microphone and inspiring a new generation into action. There are many impressive role models. They hear the song being sung by Mother Earth and they feel called to sing along.

## EARTH-SONG

Water is a popular topic. Many people are diving in and sharing their thoughts and projects about water's properties, the numerous ways it is of value to us, as well as its levels of pollution. Water is a great means of making us feel better and also clearing away what we don't need, transforming us - or rather returning us - to a different state. More evidence is indicating water's significance in a two-way relationship between its vibration and our own.

Water is the basis of all life. Drinking healthy water replenishes the body. It supports the elimination of waste and helps maintain a healthy pH level essential for the blood and our well-being. This is common knowledge, yet a growing number of people are experiencing an increase in their pH levels, partly due to food choices and partly due to chronic dehydration. Such a state provides a fertile environment for illnesses and general malaise; it also contributes to fatigue and causes pain and inflammation in the body. It is no coincidence that this change in our pH levels is occurring at the same time as the acidification of our seas. A change in the water's pH could result in devastating consequences for the lifecycle of many marine organisms, especially calcifying species such as corals, calcareous plankton and shelled organisms like oysters, mussels and clams.

Water has numerous benefits for us and on many levels; its quality and our well-being are inexorably linked. Mermaids intrinsically understand this. In my previous book, *Spiritual Seas: Diving into Life*, I pondered the notion that if eternity were contained in a grain of sand, maybe it is also contained in a drop of water. I also considered whether the sea was one entity or millions of drops. Where do the connections begin and end between water itself and also between water and ourselves? I had read about the special qualities of water and I wondered, if homeopathy worked by water having a memory of all that went before, whether the sea could hold a vision of all there was and all there was yet to be? If so, considering how much water our bodies contain, might we also hold this information?

In his many books, including perhaps his most well-known, *The Hidden Messages in Water*, the late Dr. Masaru Emoto expressed his reverence for the properties of water. Dr. Masaru Emoto, who was world-renowned for his water crystal experiments, believed that water is a type of blueprint for our reality and that our vibration, delivered through thoughts and emotions, changes the structure of water. He demonstrated that water exposed to positive vibrations produces open and clear crystals whilst negative vibrations yielded gnarled formations. As the human body contains a large percentage of water, it is easy to see how he argued that our thoughts have consequences for us at a deeply anatomical, as well as emotional, level. He stressed that the importance of positive vibrations in both our inner and outer environments cannot be over-emphasised for individuals and for humanity as a whole.

Dr. Masaru Emoto trained hundreds of instructors around the world to spread the message of *hado*. Hado, he believed, is the intrinsic vibrational pattern, at the atomic level, in all matter and is also the energy of human consciousness. Matt Thorton, a hado instructor based in the United Kingdom, looks to build and honour these teachings alongside the emerging science of water by giving people the experience of water's true nature. As we deepen into a new understanding, new foundations and paradigms of thinking about water, more of its nature and purpose are being revealed to us.

Dr. Masaru Emoto would explain to his students that the hado of water is polluted, and while Matt Thorton also expresses concern about water and the environment, he understands that all pollution can be reversed, even eradicated, albeit only at the level of understanding of hado and consciousness. Appreciating water's true nature makes the concept of pollution incomprehensible. Our infrastructure, however, is set up unconsciously to perpetuate pollution as we are conditioned to believe water is the recipient of our waste, but its true nature is exactly the opposite. Matt Thorton suggests no such crisis in water exists, only a crisis in our consciousness. A roadmap to ending pollution will be made when water is more deeply understood, ensuring the hado can be restored. Dr. Masaru Emoto believed that water is intrinsically linked to our individual and collective consciousness. His Emoto Peace Project looks to make subtle yet significant changes to our own internal environment by rising the vibration of our thoughts and our words. Matt Thorton believes this to be an exciting time as the understanding of the nature of water will take us to revisiting the foundation of science, health and medicine where, it's now known, their future will be in water, vibration, light and sound.

In his book, *The Fourth Phase of Water: Beyond Solid, Liquid, and Vapor*, Gerald H. Pollack explains how changes in water structure underlie most energetic transitions of form and motion on Earth. He believes that there is a fourth phase of water, more viscous, dense, and alkaline than regular water. This "living water" has a negative charge and can hold and deliver energy. He explains that this is not $H_2O$, but $H_3O_2$, known as EZ water (exclusion zone). He argues the water in our cells is not regular water, but highly structured water with special properties. His work has added to the value of reappraising our assumptions of what it means to have water within and around us.

MJ Pangman and Melanie Evans, authors of *Dancing with Water: The New Science of Water*, have further expanded the conversation about water's multifaceted role in life on this planet, particularly as a vehicle for the transmission of energy and information and as a conscious participant in, what they coin, "the dance of life." In their book, they discuss the water's liquid crystalline phase and its biological significance for us. They acknowledge the connection between matter and spirit. They explain that we can naturally, treat, structure, energise and revitalise the water we use by adding appropriate information to it. By so doing, we connect with Mother Earth and water, the lifeblood of the planet, and will then hear the Earth-Song once more.

With evidence mounting about how precious water is, both internally and externally, it's vital to release our negative thoughts by diving deep into our blue minds to keep our waters clean. The mirrors of life seem clear: heal our lives and heal our planet. As mermaids, we want to dive deep into this conversation adding to the expanding ripple of awareness of such an important concept.

## SEA-ING YOUR LIFE DIFFERENTLY

It is remarkable when you realise that what you had previously considered to be your defects are actually your strengths. More than remarkable, it is life-changing, resulting in a fundamental shift in your self-esteem, your decision-making process and your willingness to engage in life. You almost hear your inner mermaid clapping as you have finally realised what she knew all the time: that your life is a gift. She has been waiting your whole life for you to realise your value, own your power and to start to play, co-creating with the

Universe, expanding it, nurturing it, protecting it with your loving energy. Consider:

- Trying something new, just because you can.

- Reconnecting with old friends and returning to well-loved, but neglected hobbies.

- Claiming your place within the sisterhood and offering a hand to Mother Earth.

## CREST OF A WAVE

This chapter explained the interconnectivity of life and looks at the importance of helping yourself, being helped and offering service to your community. The ripple effect of this is beyond our imagination and it starts one splash at a time.

The final chapter is a review of the concepts covered in the book. Most importantly, it reminds you of your choice to take action and offers strategies and tools to engage with.

## MERMAID MINDSET

*I lose if I am the only one that wins.*

Mermaids understand the connectedness of life and the part they play within it. I heard of a workplace team-building exercise in which the participants were split into teams and each person within a team was given a balloon and a pin. The team that managed to keep their balloons from being popped would be the winners. Within minutes, the room was filled with people defending their own balloons and attacking their colleagues' balloons. After a number of attempts they realised that there would be no winners if they continued to approach the task this way, just a mass of debris on the floor. The solution was to agree that no one would attack and for each to honour the agreement. This was the goal of the team-building exercise. Maybe it's the same for humanity.

## MERMAID MOTTOS

Before you journal, write some mermaid mottos. You are welcome to use mine.

> *I am willing to believe in myself.*
>
> *I believe in humanity.*
>
> *I celebrate Mother Earth.*

## EXERCISE

### RANDOM ACTS OF KINDNESS

A valued spiritual practice across different faiths is the act of random kindness. This act is unexpected by the receiver, be it a friend, stranger or Mother Earth. It can consist of practical, emotional or financial assistance; it can be picking up litter, cleaning up a beach, or offering someone a smile or a kind word. Whatever form it takes, this strategy reaps many rewards for the giver, the receiver and humanity as a whole. A sense of well-being results from feeling that you have made a difference to the lives of others. Random acts of kindness may start as a conscious practice, but in time it becomes a way of living. Begin to notice:

- When an act of kindness is given to you.

- When you automatically give it to someone else.

- When you seized an opportunity to offer someone or something a kindness and when you didn't. Also notice the times you were not even aware the opportunity existed until it had already passed.

**SEA-C**

COMMUNITY

There are times when we want to be alone, but there are times we benefit from being in groups. Finding a community that inspires you and that you can offer support to is rewarding. Consider where you could make a difference, for example, a rowing group or a conservation group.

*I enjoy the positive outcomes of collective contribution.*

*I value my sense of community and connection when I am of service to others.*

# CHAPTER 9: SURFING

*A space to journal my thoughts from this chapter…*

# A CONSIDERATION

What would you like to experience in this life?

_____

_____


What would you like to be remembered for?

_____

_____


What are your strengths and do you use these to contribute to others?

_____

_____


If you could grant the world one wish what would it be?

_____

_____


If you could make one difference in the world what would it be?

_____

_____

# COMMITMENT AND MY PLAN OF ACTION

What act of random kindness will I commit to giving today?

_____

_____

_____

What plan of action will I make to ensure I give service to my
Earth community?

_____

_____

_____

_____

_____

_____

_____

_____

_____

_____

_____

_____

_____

_____

*I commit. Signed:* _____

# Chapter Ten

## THE MERMAID'S SONG

*"When you have swam in the sea*

*a lake will no longer do;*

*everyone else has been a pond*

*but the ocean was always you."*

— *-Tyler Knott Gregson-*

## MERMAIDS SINGING

W hen there is appreciation of our deeper psyche we are more able to navigate our life experiences. We have the understanding of what to release and what to establish so we can keep our vibration high. This does not mean labels encompass who you are, only that you use them to understand yourself better and cherish your traits. Once you appreciate who you are and how you protect, restore, maintain and utilise your energy you are better placed to have the energy you need for your enjoyment and assignment on Earth.

## FOR SHORE

How can you live on planet Earth using only your five senses and believe that is all there is? How can there be any doubt when you have seen the invisible, heard the unspoken and felt the eternal? As mermaids would never be happy contained in a lake, a pool or anywhere but the sea, we Earthlings will continue to hear our soul's calling until our inner selves have been set free from our restrictions. By doing so we then hear Mother Earth celebrating the harmonic and harmonious nature of creation.

It felt crystal clear to me as I swam back to the boat. Information can empower, as can having trust that you are guided. There are many ways to the same destination and many starting points. There is so much information available if we ask, search and are aware. Everything communicates something special. Some self-help messages focus on our thoughts, our emotions or our beliefs; others, on our physical bodies or on our dreams or dramas. How we are inspired into action and what comment or insight resonates within us is for us to discover. By doing so, we support the collective mission of clearing the consciousness of the whole. If water is our planet's lifeblood, then mermaids swim as messengers of peace.

I had jumped into the realm of the mermaid with the need for total immersion. As I resurfaced I could see what remnants of water bounced off like diamonds, dropped like tears or clung, leaving salty patches as they dried. I knew I was responsible for many of my experiences and I wanted to understand this better and play with the energy. It felt too important to be left to chance. We decide whether to dive deep and explore who we are and how we respond to internal and external stimuli. We have a choice whether to change our perception and explore the conversations in our head, and having done so, whether we repeat the same patterns in our relationships with others and ourselves or if we want to experience something else. First we need to be aware of that choice and what we are presently doing. From this basis we can engage in the process of change more consciously. When we vibrate at a higher frequency we support change in the consciousness of humanity.

I was fascinated by all the information available supporting self-awareness, although the way it was delivered did not always resonate with me. Specific instructions, especially if given in authoritarian ways, resulted in my withdrawal. Spotlights, being questioned for specific answers, loud groups or being expected to follow set criteria made me feel uneasy. The best approach I discovered was not following a path already made, but swimming along a channel of my own, with the latitude to change my direction as and when guided to do so.

One of the most effective strategies for getting in the right channel is to know yourself. By doing so you are aware of what gives you energy and a vibrational high and what takes it away. Another is appreciating the laws of manifestation to support you in achieving your dreams, especially if coupled with an equal belief in miracles to help the process flow. My dream is to swim in crystal clear waters again, and to feel the water wrap around me like a mother's arms wrap around a daughter who has finally come home.

I have learnt much from the concept of my mermaid who, for me, encompasses the qualities of an empath and an introvert and who feels the memory of eternity in her soul. I know she will resonate with others and she will guide us to swim together. The mermaids are our soul friends. Being with people who understand us can further help our ability to sing our song. The mermaid has a strong calling, not to be in the limelight for fame, but to make a difference by appeasing the friction on Earth. The mermaids reach out their hands in the strong currents and urge us to return home, back to the peace and calm. The mermaids won't dictate, they won't save you, but they offer an invitation for you to accept whenever you are ready, to value the light in yourself once more.

## THE MERMAID'S WAY

My mind leapt in amazement. The sea was again showing me how beautiful the world is when nature reveals itself in all its glory. With every turn the water offered a new realm of beauty. Each layer of the sea has its own unique fish and marine life that are perfectly matched for their habitat. As I dived deeper I could see, from the abundance and variety of gloriously coloured fish, that the wave action was no longer a concern. The amazing caves and overhangs full of soft corals helped to set the stage for a spectacular show. The exquisite aquatic dancers in their colourful costumes swayed to the rhythms of the sea, almost as if performing choreographed movements to delight spectators. As the coral communities change with increasing depth so does our inner landscape and the inner work it uncovers for us. It is an ongoing process. There is always more to learn and there is always deeper to dive. Life is our journey towards understanding and empowerment, a navigation towards peace and love and feeling at ease with the part we play in the eternal flow of life.

During a recent dive in the Maldives, the tide changed and the current suddenly got stronger, seemingly from several directions at once. The divers were taken all over the place, and even the most experienced were surfacing with shaken egos and very little air left in their tanks. As with the sea, life presents the unexpected. Not all events are welcome, but how we move with life can influence whether we struggle or flow. Indeed, life will present unexpected opportunities to shine a light on new areas for healing, best undertaken through thoughtful reflection of your inner and outer worlds.

On another dive elsewhere, we were spat out on the sea's surface by an up-current a long way from the boat that was to pick us up. One of our group reported that this had happened to him before and had resulted in a rather anxious wait of over an hour before he was picked up. He had learnt from the experience and as a consequence he had brought a strobe light with him on this dive and so our drama was quickly resolved. The torch flash caught the necessary attention of those on the boat, the way that light usually does.

## CELEBRATORY MERMAIDS

Once you understand who you are, you can give yourself permission to shine. You have more strategies to help protect and recharge your energy, to bounce back from setbacks and to motivate you to take the necessary action for change as required. You have a healthy inner voice and healthier boundaries. You feel more validated and worthy of being of service to others.

As you dive deeper you are appreciative of the support available to assist you through the waves of your life. By understanding yourself better, you are happier in your own skin and more confident to stand on your stage of life. You are better placed to help others and there is an enhanced quality of interaction between you and those in your world. You begin to enjoy interactions more, even feeling that it is your purpose to shine as brightly as possible during every interaction you have, resulting in a ripple effect across the Universe that surprises us all.

## MOMENTARY MERMAIDS

The mermaid is a helpful label and I am grateful for it. In the short term it can help us understand ourselves better. It does not, however, define us. As *A Course in Miracles* explains, there is only love and all we need to do is remember this.

In the end we discard our labels and come as we are. We are unique and yet no more or no less than anyone else. We swim in the sea of humanity, navigating the currents and the waves, floating with our dreams and struggling or sinking with any excess baggage we decide to hold. In the end, when we let go of it all, we become one indistinguishable part of the whole. We are all destined to return home. Only then will the mermaid release her sparkles fully and they will hit the water's surface for the last time and bounce into the air, demonstrating and celebrating how wonderful we always were.

## MERMAID MODE

*Mermaids are comfortable with their shine.*

Mermaids are here to shine their light on the beauty of humankind, living on a planet of abundance.

## WAVE HELLO AND WAVE GOODBYE

As we conclude our time together, I feel it's helpful to include the following memory aid. Consider which points are the most relevant for you and which you want to engage with first.

- Wave hello to your inner mermaid.
- Wave goodbye to self-sabotaging behaviour.
- Wave hello to affirmations.
- Wave goodbye to blame.

- Wave hello to self-care.

- Wave goodbye to old stories that no longer serve you.

- Wave hello to forgiveness.

- Wave goodbye to harsh judgements.

- Wave hello to giving miracles a chance.

- Wave goodbye to clutter.

- Wave hello to miracles!

## SEA-ING YOUR LIFE DIFFERENTLY

As you close this book, what will you take away? What have you learnt, remembered or dismissed? All responses offer an insight into where you are and where you could explore further.

- What do you want to adjust in your life and how will you start?

- Will you immerse yourself into your day with love or fear?

## CREST OF A WAVE

This chapter summarised the importance of personal awareness. Through the mermaids we allow ourselves to play with life again and find a happier flow. By being in harmony with your true self you are better positioned to add to the ripple effect occurring within you and across the sea of life.

The mermaid represents the ultimate inner child, as well as the fractious psyche of the personal and global unconscious. This mermaid dances to the tune of eternal mystery, as enduring as love itself, residing in the bloodline of our planet and singing along with the Earth-Song.

## MERMAID MINDSET

*I forget so I can remember all over again.*

When we remember that we are more than our stories, our shortcomings and our dramas, we can ride the waves of our life with more joy. We find grace in everyday moments and help others along the way. When we release and forget past judgements and beliefs that hold us back, we remember again that life is a precious gift. The ripple effect is as vast as the sea itself.

## MERMAID MOTTOS

Before you journal, create some mermaid mottos for your ongoing journey.

*I am powerful and I choose to live in love.*

*I am clearer about who I am and what I want to give and receive.*

*I am part of the loving Universe.*

## EXERCISE

TAKE THE PLUNGE, DIP YOUR TOE, GET WET

There is a lot of information in this book. Some parts will resonate with you more than others.

* Take time to be specific and map out what you want to wave hello to and what you want to wave goodbye to.
* Make notes to act as your memory aid and to organise your thoughts.
* Create your plan of action.
* Make your commitment.
* Take the necessary action.

As we divers say, "Plan your dive, then dive your plan!"

## SEA-C

## COMMITMENT

To commit to something, especially if accompanied by your signature, sends a strong message to both yourself and the Universe that you are ready. Sign your plan of action, write your lists and dates and add necessary content to your diary. As you start the process, be aware of any signs and synchronicities. Recognise that life is presenting you with support and be willing to take further action.

*When I commit to paper I take the necessary action to make it happen.*

*When I take the necessary action I invite the power of the Universe to flow through me.*

*When I dive into myself with compassion I discover treasures and my enjoyment for life.*

# CHAPTER 10: THE MERMAID'S SONG

*A space to journal my thoughts from this chapter…*

# A CONSIDERATION

Read the quotes below and make notes on any that rock your boat.

"I alone cannot change the world, but I can cast a stone across the waters to create many ripples."

— **Mother Teresa**

"We can't be afraid of change. You may feel very secure in the pond that you are in, but if you never venture out of it, you will never know that there is such a thing as an ocean, a sea. Holding onto something that is good for you now, may be the very reason why you don't have something better."

— **C. JoyBell C.**

"The world as we have created it is a process of our thinking. It cannot be changed without changing our thinking."

— **Albert Einstein**

"Stepping onto a brand-new path is difficult, but not more difficult than remaining in a situation which is not nurturing to the whole woman."

— **Maya Angelou**

# COMMITMENT AND MY PLAN OF ACTION

What constructive action will I commit to doing or taking today to support my goals?

_____

_____

_____

What is my long-term plan of action?

_____

_____

_____

_____

_____

_____

_____

_____

_____

_____

_____

_____

_____

_____

_____

_____

*I commit. Signed:* _____

# Epilogue

## THE MERMAIDS ARE HERE

*"Your soul is so bohemian, free and gypsy wild. Come swim with me in the calming sea, let's be mermaids for awhile."*

**— Melody Lee, *Moon Gypsy***

## THE DIVINE FEMININE IS HERE

There are superstars dancing in our midst in ever-increasing numbers. Maybe you know one or are one. This energy values the yin and the yang, yet sings of the importance of the collective as opposed to the competitive, the belief in empowerment over control, in abundance rather than scarcity and a belief in love over fear. This energy is here to remind us of our power, activated through love. It is changing our planet's consciousness one heart after another.

## THE INVITATION

There is a great deal to congratulate and endorse in our world and much is possible when we are in harmony. However, for a time our planet seems to have been out of harmony and separation and fear appeared to be increasing.

The mermaid's return is to remind us of the importance of reflection and of diving deep to support a clearer perspective of the larger picture and the inter-connectedness of us all. The mermaids sing again, inviting us all to remember the Earth-Song.

## THE PARTY

There is a renewed energy looking at how we do business, educate and care, as well as how we live our lives with more harmony, ensuring sustainability.

Many of us are still in the current of change, unsure of the outcome and our final destination, still reacting rather than choosing and allowing. Many people still believe what they have been told rather than diving into their own eternal truth.

All is not lost; help is at hand. It's been here all along, swimming deep with grace and curiosity within us all, watching and waiting for the time. And the time is now.

The mermaids have arrived with an outward sparkle that reflects our inner shine and our authentic spirit, however deep these reside. Whereas once they too would have hidden their sparkle for fear of being misunderstood, today they know there is no more time to wait. They shine their beauty on the stage of your life.

This energy is contained in all forms, old and the young, scared and the intrepid. It is also a timeless reflection of your wisdom and your heart, rather than a physical attribute subject to change. It is the beauty that allures from within. It is the wisdom of all time that honours both the land and the sea and the love that transcends us all.

The mermaids open their hearts and their arms and encourage us Earthlings, with cosmic hearts, to unite once more to sing our universal-song.

# PART MOON AND SUN

"Everybody has a little bit of the sun and moon in them.
Everybody has a little bit of man, woman, and animal in them.
Darks and lights in them.

Everyone is part of a connected cosmic system. Part earth and sea,
wind and fire, with some salt and dust swimming in them.

We have a universe within ourselves that mimics
the universe outside.

None of us are just black or white, or never wrong
and always right.

No one. No one exists without polarities."


**— Suzy Kassem, Rise Up and Salute the Sun: The Writings of
Suzy Kassem**

# THE CHORUS

So gently they sang,

in harmony with each other,

their voices hardly audible,

but the vibration increased considerably

so much so

that change was inevitable.

Where as before they had to contain their beauty

scared of captivity,

now there was no other option but to reveal the outward shine of
their glorious hearts,

and to offer the gifts of eternal truth.

They have joined forces with the sisters.

So now,

the mermaids sing again.

This time they will succeed

in giving the gifts they want to share.

They sprinkle their sparkle on the human form

engaging an audience ready to shine,

mesmerising and stirring a memory in each high priestess,

reminding a new generation of who they really are

and of their power to transform

our age.

**Tonia Browne**

# ACKNOWLEDGEMENTS

I would like to acknowledge and thank many wonderful people who have helped make *Mermaids: An Empath and Introvert's Guide to Riding the Waves of Life,* and the Diving into Life series, possible.

To Mum and Dad, for giving me many adventures and loving me always. To Julian, for taking me with him on many diving escapades, for giving me the time and encouragement to write, and for his constant love. Thanks also to my wonderful sister, Niki, who finds time for me, even during the busiest of occasions. To Faye and Ryan, a reminder of the miracle of life and the courage of the next generation.

To Patricia Crane who supported me through my first Heal Your Life® Workshop experience and my subsequent HYL training. To the late Louise Hay and the Hay House Community for their tireless endeavours to help hearts, souls and minds find love through their inspirational stories and practical advice.

To Marco Busoni, for creating and allowing me to use his beautiful mermaid painting on the front cover of this book. I fell in love with her instantly.

Thank you to Jase White for taking the photo of me and capturing me in a good light.

To Shanda Trofe, my Authorpreneur, who helped me float through the writing and publishing process by giving such useful practical and emotional support. She is a legend in her own lifetime.

Thank you to Dana Micheli for her attention to detail and consideration when editing my work. Her polishing gave it an extra shine.

To Melodie and Shona, two goddess friends who entice me out of my shell to party whenever they think I've been in there too long. To Luci, Suzy, Helen, Helena and Kim, I'd be a lesser human without our walks and talks! To Tracy and Alison, my forever friends. To Vandana and Julie for our many lifetimes. To Katrin and Matt and synchronicity. To Pat and all our adventures. To Allegra who taught me more than she will ever know, and to those that showed me love and courage in action.

To Clare, who showed me there is a book in all of us and it can be written. To Lisa Hardwick, who gave me my first writing opportunity and many more thereafter. She had faith in me until I had my own.

To Jane and my wonderful diving buddies, and to the crew and staff on many diving adventures - thank you for your encouragement and helping hands.

To my friends in so many lifetimes who kept the light shining for me in this one.

To all the many wonderful people I have encountered in my life and have still to meet.

Thanks again to Patricia and Shanda, along with much gratitude to Ali Day, Damien Munro, Sneha Shah, Shashank Gupta and Sunny Dawn Johnston who gave their supportive energy to this book. I am forever grateful.

# BIBLIOGRAPHY

Anderson, R. Charles. *Reef Fishes of the Maldives.* Manta Marine; reprint edition, 2005

Ashley, Katie. *How Multi-Passionate Female Entrepreneurs Are Changing The World.* 2017 https://www.huffingtonpost.com/katie-ashley/how-multi-passionate-female-entrepreneurs-are-changing-the-world_b_9244374.html

Bernstein, Gabrielle. https://gabbybernstein.com

Braden, Gregg. T*he Divine Matrix: Bridging Time, Space, Miracles, and Belief.* Hay House Inc., 2008

Brown, Brené. *Braving the Wilderness: The Quest For True Belonging and the Courage to Stand Alone.* Random House, 2017

Browne, Tonia. *Spiritual Seas: Diving Into Life.* Transcendent Publishing, 2016

Buelow, Beth. theintrovertsenrepreneur.com

Cain, Susan. quietrev.com

Cain, Susan. *Quiet: The Power of Introverts in a World That Can't Stop Talking.* Broadway Books, 2013

Cain, Susan. QUIZ: Are You an Introvert or an Extrovert? (And Why It Matters) The north and south of temperament. Posted Mar 09, 2011 Psychology Today: https://www.psychologytoday.com/blog/quiet-the-power-introverts/201103/quiz-are-you-introvert-or-extrovert-and-why-it-matters and TED TALK https://www.ted.com/talks/susan_cain_the_power_of_introverts February 2012

Coleman, Neville. *Marine Life of the Maldives.* James Bennett Pty Ltd, 2000

Corter, Melissa. https://melissacorter.com

Crane, Patricia J. *Ordering from the Cosmic Kitchen: The Essential Guide to Powerful, Nourishing Affirmations.* Health Horizon, 2012 and www.orderingfromthecosmickitchen.com

De Vee, Gina. https://divineliving.com

Duffield-Thomas, Denise. https://luckybitch.com

Dyer, Wayne. *Excuses Begone! How to Change Lifelong, Self-Defeating Thinking Habits.* Hay House Inc, 2010

Emote, Masaru. *The Hidden Messages in Water. Beyond Words* Publishing Inc, 2004 and Secret Life of Water Beyond. Words Publishing Inc, 2006 and http://www.masaru-emoto.net/english/water-crystal.html

Estés, Clarissa Pinkola. *Women who Run with the Wolves: Myths and Stories of the Wild Woman Archetype.* Ballantine Books, 1995

Forleo, Marie. https://www.marieforleo.com

Foundation for Inner Peace. *A Course in Miracles.* 2008

Hay House Wisdom Community. http://www.hayhouse.co.uk/wisdom/

Hay, Louise. Official Website. http://www.hayhouse.com and http://www.louisehay.com/about/

Hay, Louise. *You Can Heal Your Life.* Hay House Inc., 1984

HYL Training. http://www.healyourlifetraining.com/teacher-training/

Hay House I Can Conference. http://www.hayhouse.co.uk/lectures-events/event-tours

Heer, Dain. Access Consciousness.
http://www.accessconsciousness.com

Hendricks, Gay. *The Big Leap: Conquer Your Hidden Fear and Take Life to the Next Level.* HarperCollins, 2010 and Hendricks, Gay. https://hendricks.com

Hicks, Esther and Jerry. *Ask and it is Given: Learning to Manifest The Law of Attraction.* Hay House Inc,2008 and http://www.abraham-hicks.com

Hauser-Carson, Carolin. www.thepleasurewhisperer.com

Iflscience. *Watching Fish Is Good For Your Health.* http://www.iflscience.com/health-and-medicine/watching-fish-good-your-health/

Johnston, Sunny Dawn. https://sunnydawnjohnston.com

Kim, W C. and Mauborgne, R. *Blue Ocean Strategy: How to Create Uncontested Market Space and Make the Competition Irrelevant.* Boston, Mass, Harvard Business School Press, 2005

Kim, W C. and Mauborgne, R. *Blue Ocean Shift: Beyond Competing - Proven Steps to Inspire Confidence and Seize New Growth.* Hachette Books, 2017

Kuiter, Rudie Hermann. *Fishes of the Maldives: Indian Ocean.* Atoll Publishing, Australia, 2014

Lipton, Bruce. *The Biology of Belief: Unleashing the Power of Consciousness, Matter & Miracles.* Hay House Inc., 2008 and https://www.brucelipton.com

Linn, Denise. *The Secret Language of Signs: How to Interpret the Coincidences and Symbols of Life.* Ballantine Book Publishing, NY, 1996 and http://www.deniselinn.com

Lomax, Richard. *The Ocean's Cleaners*
https://www.thenakedscientists.com/articles/features/oceans-cleaners

Luniw, Karen. *Personal & Business Mindset Expert.*
http://www.thelawofattractioncenter.com/questfirmations-putting-you-into-the-space-of-having-what-you-want/

Myss, Caroline. https://www.myss.com

Myss, Caroline. *Archetypes: Who Are You?* Audiobook, Hay House Inc, 2013

Nichols, Wallace J. *Blue Mind: The Surprising Science That Shows How Being Near, In, On, or Under Water Can Make You Happier, Healthier, More Connected, and Better at What You Do.* Back Bay Books, 2015

Northrup, Christine. https://www.drnorthrup.com

Orloff, Judith. *The Empath's Survival Guide: Life Strategies for Sensitive People.* Sounds True, 2017

Palmer, Alison. www.fullcirclewomen.com

Pangman, MJ. and Evans, Melanie. *Dancing with Water: The New Science of Water.* 2011and http://www.dancingwithwater.com

Perry, J. Mitchell. *The Road to Optimism: Change Your Language—Change Your Life!* Tantalus Books, San Ramon, CA, Fort Collins, CO 1996

Pollack, Gerald H. *The Fourth Phase of Water: Beyond Solid, Liquid, Vapor.* University of Washington, 2013

National Geographic. Ocean Acidification. 2017
https://www.nationalgeographic.com/environment/oceans/critical-issues-ocean-acidification/

http://ocean.si.edu/ocean-acidification

Olivera, Makarena. socialintroverts.com

Richardson, Cheryl. *The Art of Extreme Self-Care: Transform Your Life One Month at a Time.* Hay House Inc., 2012

Robbins, Mel. https://melrobbins.com/blog/the-5-second-rule/

Sandon, Melissa. https://melissasandon.com

Summerhawk, Kendall. http://www.kendallsummerhawk.com

Thornton, Matt. www.newwatergeneration.com and www.NWGcommercial.com

Vitale, Joe and Ihaleakala, Hew Len. *Zero Limits: The Secret Hawaiian System for Wealth, Health, Peace, and More.* John Wiley & Sons, Inc., Hoboken, New Jersey, 2007

Weaver, Libby. drlibby.com

Weaver, Libby. TEDx Presentation Crisis In Women's Health https://www.youtube.com/watch?time_continue=33&v=tJ0SME6Z9rw TEDxQueenstown 2014

Weaver, Libby. https://www.drlibby.com/stress/slowing-down-the-ageing-process/?utm_source=drip&utm_medium=email&utm_campaign=Ageing+from+the+inside+out#australia

Williamson, Marianne. *A Return to Love: Reflections on the Principles of a Course in Miracles.* HarperCollins, 1996 and https://marianne.com

Williamson, Marianne. *The Aphrodite Training: On the Convergence of Woman, Goddess, and Lover* https://marianne.com/the-aphrodite-training-2/

All starting quotes were accessed from Goodreads.com https://www.goodreads.com/

***Declaimer: The websites were correct at the time of publishing.

# ABOUT THE AUTHOR

Tonia Browne is a bestselling author, teacher and coach. She is a strong advocate of inviting fun into our lives and encouraging people to see their world from a new perspective.

Tonia's writing includes coaching strategies interspersed with spiritual insights and personal anecdotes. She takes a holistic approach to change and believes in liberating the inner child within each of us.

As a teacher, Tonia has worked in the United Kingdom and internationally for over twenty years and was an Assistant Head for seven. In addition to her mainstream training as a teacher, she is a Heal Your Life® Workshop Leader, Coach and Business Trainer.

Tonia's first solo book, Spiritual Seas: *Diving into Life: 12 Strategies for Riding the Waves of Life,* reached Amazon Number 1 Ranking in both the USA and the UK. Her next book, *Mermaids: A Playful Companion*, is a journal full of colouring pages, inspiration and practical exercises to support an inner dive for outer sparkle. It makes a perfect companion to this book and can also stand alone.

Check out Tonia's website for her collection of *Mermaids Diving into Life* cards, a beautiful trilogy of images and statements to help you dive into your own life and to keep you uplifted. Also look at the range of Mermaid Apparel to keep their energy with you all day.

Connect with Tonia @ toniabrowne.com.

CPSIA information can be obtained
at www.ICGtesting.com
Printed in the USA
BVHW041323160719
553580BV00016B/948/P